USING COMPUTERS

Do you want to learn about computers? Or
understand more about how to program
your microcomputer? Then this book is a
good place to start.

The various units of a computer and the
principles of programming are simply and
clearly explained. Then there are chapters
dealing with the different applications of
computers, ranging from playing games to
data processing. USING COMPUTERS
also explains how robots work, the
different ways of communicating with
computers, and the importance of
computer security.

The collection of programs for you to use
yourself makes learning about computers
enormous fun for everyone, young and old.

About the authors:

Lionel Carter is a qualified Chartered Mechanical Engineer. He is a Principal Lecturer in Management Science at Slough College of Higher Education. He has given lectures on computers, decision making and related topics at Birmingham University, Brunel University, the Civil Service Staff College, EITB, Henley Staff College and the National Water Industry Council.

Eva Huzan is the Head of the Computing Division at Slough College of Higher Education, having previously worked as a physicist and computing lecturer in industry. She has carried out research at two University of London Colleges, gaining PhD degrees in Solid State Physics and in Computing. She is a member of several advisory panels concerned with computer education, and is a committee member of the British Computer Society Microcomputer Specialist Group.

The authors have collaborated before in writing a number of books, including *The Pocket Calculator*, *Computer Programming in BASIC*, and *Microelectronics and Microcomputers* all published by Teach Yourself Books.

USING COMPUTERS

Lionel Carter and Eva Huzan

KNIGHT BOOKS
Hodder and Stoughton

Text and illustrations copyright © L. R. Carter and E. Huzan 1982
First published by Knight Books 1982

British Library C.I.P.

Carter, Lionel
  Using computers.
  1. Computers – Juvenile literature
  2. Electronic data processing – Juvenile literature
  I. Title   II. Huzan, Eva
  001.64   QA76.23

  ISBN 0-340-32062-1

I would like to thank my two sons, Nicholas and Peter, for their contribution to the preparation of this book.

Eva Huzan

Printed and bound in Great Britain for Hodder and
Stoughton Paperbacks, a division of Hodder and
Stoughton Ltd., Mill Road, Dunton Green, Sevenoaks,
Kent (Editorial Office: 47 Bedford Square, London, WC1
3DP) by Richard Clay Ltd. (The Chaucer Press), Bungay, Suffolk.
Photoset by Rowland Phototypesetting Ltd.,
Bury St Edmunds, Suffolk.

Contents

List of Figures

List of Tables

How To Use This Book

This book is different from other books you may have seen on how computers are used. It contains actual programs for you to try out on a microcomputer.

If you are new to computing, start by reading Chapters 1 and 2 to learn about computer equipment and programming. You can then choose any chapter to read about a particular application. There are chapters on playing games and drawing charts and pictures, robots and communicating with computers, computer security and data processing.

You can read about the application, enter the programs into the microcomputer, and run them to get a better understanding of that use of computers. The programs have been designed to run on Commodore VIC microcomputers, and hints for converting programs to other microcomputers are given in Appendix B.

Two things need to be mentioned before you continue reading. Firstly, the terms used throughout the computer industry generally have the American form of spelling: disk instead of disc, program instead of programme, and so on. Secondly, there are two useful glossaries at the end of the book – one (on p. 113) describing the terms used in the computer programming language BASIC, which is used throughout the book, the other (on p. 141) describing the specific meanings of the words and phrases which are used generally throughout the industry. Whenever you find you can't understand a phrase or a BASIC instruction, you should refer to these glossaries.

1 How Computers Work

The units of a computer

Computers were once called also by an alternative name – stored-program computers. The latter name shows one of the main features of a computer, which is its ability to obey stored sequences of instructions without the user of the computer intervening. This sequence of instructions is called a computer program. Once the user has given a command to the computer to start executing a program, the computer will continue to obey the programmed instructions until it comes to the end of the program or until it comes to an instruction it cannot obey (this will cause what is known as an execution error).

The program has to be stored in the computer's memory (also called the main store) while its instructions are being obeyed. You may want to use a number of different programs. These can be stored on secondary or backing storage devices which usually use magnetic tape or disk. When you want to use a particular program that is stored on tape or disk, it is necessary to load it from the tape or disk into the computer's memory. The action of loading a program causes the program's instructions to be copied into the computer's memory; the tape or disk remains unchanged.

Your program may call for information to be entered – two values to be added together in an addition instruction, for instance. This information needed by the program, the two values in this particular case, is known as data. The data may be entered on a keyboard, which may look like part of a typewriter or may have touch-sensitive keys. Such an entry device is known as an input device. If your program is processing a lot of data, as would be required for a business application designed, say, to process orders or invoices, it would be inconvenient and slow to input the data as required from a keyboard. In such cases, the data would be held as files of data on magnetic tape or disk. The computer would read the data from the file as directed by the program.

Once a program is in the memory, the computer needs to be able to work on the data. This is done in the arithmetic and logic unit (ALU). The ALU takes the data to be processed from the memory, does the required calculation according to the program instruction, and then puts the result back into the memory.

Results have to be displayed in some form that is understandable to the user. They may be printed on a printer or displayed on a visual display unit (VDU). A VDU has a screen similar to your television set's. Several personal or home computers, such as the Commodore VIC, use an ordinary television for the screen display.

A computer is a complex piece of electronic equipment that is capable of processing data very quickly. The processing power of large computers is often quoted in millions of instructions that can be processed per second (mips). The

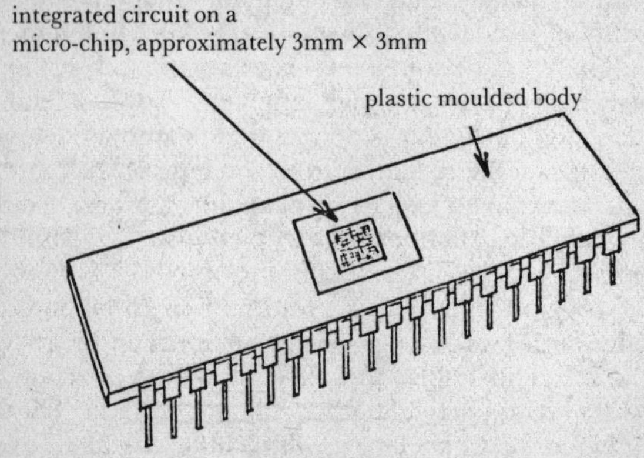

integrated circuit on a
micro-chip, approximately 3mm × 3mm

plastic moulded body

Figure 1.1   A micro-chip (integrated circuit)

various parts of the computer send and receive signals at electronic speeds, and it is vital that the speeds and synchronization of the signals are accurately controlled. This is the function of the control unit.

The central part of the computer – memory, arithmetic and logic unit, and control unit – is known as its central processor or central processing unit (CPU). It is possible to have the circuits required for a central processor built into a single chip, usually made from silicon and known as a silicon chip. Such chips are called microprocessors. A micro-chip (integrated circuit) is shown in Figure 1.1.

A microprocessor may have only a limited amount of memory, and this may need to be extended by the use of additional memory chips, as described in Hardware on page 6. It is possible to have a complete small microcomputer that uses only a single chip. These microcomputer chips can

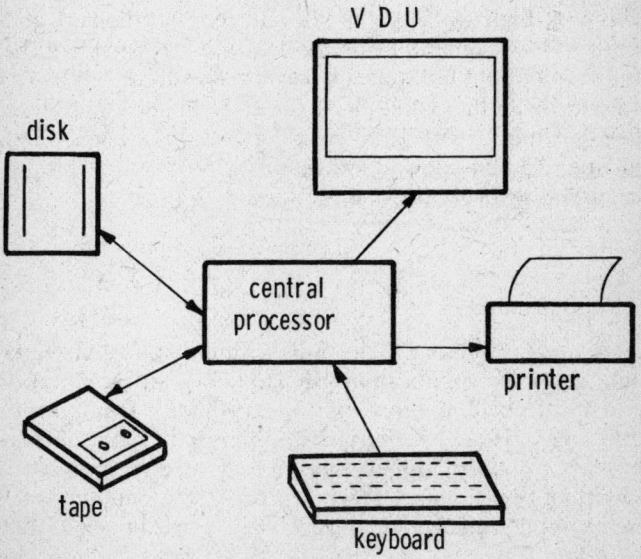

Figure 1.2   Units of a typical microcomputer system

even be used to control industrial or domestic equipment, such as washing and sewing machines and stereo systems. The type of microcomputer system discussed in this book is shown in Figure 1.2. Similar units are used with larger computers. The processor can read data from or direct data to a cassette tape unit or a disk unit, and can display output on a visual display unit or send it to a printer. Many personal computers, such as the Commodore vic, include the central processor (microprocessor chip) circuitry and main memory in the keyboard unit.

The binary system

Information is stored in computers in binary form. Binary digits have either the value one or zero and can be represented within the computer by just two states, examples of which are high and low levels of voltage or north-south and south-north magnetic fields. Any two-state system can be used to represent the zero and one binary values.

Binary counting is similar to counting in decimal but, as there are only two digits, carrying is required more frequently. Adding one and one in binary results in a carry of one to the next column; that is

$$\begin{array}{r} 1 \\ \underline{1} \\ 10 \end{array} (= \text{decimal } 2)$$

Continuing to add one to the previous number up to decimal eight gives the results shown in Table 1.1. In the decimal system each column represents powers of ten – that is, units (10^0), tens (10^1), hundreds (10^2), thousands (10^3), and so on – whereas in the binary system each column represents powers of two – that is, units (2^0), twos (2^1), fours (2^2), etc. For example, you can find the decimal value of binary 110 as follows:

```
        1  0        ( = decimal 2 )
           1
        1  1        ( = decimal 3 )
           1
     1  0  0        ( = decimal 4 )
           1
     1  0  1        ( = decimal 5 )
           1
     1  1  0        ( = decimal 6 )
           1
     1  1  1        ( = decimal 7 )
           1
  1  0  0  0        ( = decimal 8 )
```

Table 1.1 Binary addition

column value	2^2	2^1	2^0	
binary	1	1	0	
decimal	4 +	2 +	0	= 6

This shows that binary code 110 is equivalent to decimal 6.

Zero and one binary digits are called bits (from *b*inary dig*its*). Therefore, 110 is a three-bit number. The term byte (pronounced 'bite') is used to mean a group of eight bits, and much of computer circuitry is designed to process information in bytes. With some computers the unit of data handled by the circuitry is a word, which is usually made up of several bytes. For example, a 32-bit word is made up of four bytes.

All the letters of the alphabet, other characters such as punctuation, and numbers have to be coded into binary before the computer can make use of them. A commonly used code is the ASCII code (American Standard Code for Information Interchange). In this code, the letter A, for example, is 1000001. An extra bit is added for checking purposes, making eight bits in all. There are several other coding systems in use, but the ASCII code is the one most frequently used with microcomputers.

	DATA :	3 PIES
DATA		**ASCII**
3		0110011
(space)		0100000
P		1010000
I		1001001
E		1000101
S		1010011

Table 1.2   Some data coded into binary

In general, then, an item of data or information is coded into ASCII code character by character, including spaces, as shown in Table 1.2. Now that you know how data can be stored and processed, we can consider in more detail some aspects of computer equipment.

Hardware

All the physical items of the computer system, i.e. those that can be seen, are called 'hardware'. The programs, whether stored on tape or disk or in main memory, are called 'software' as opposed to hardware.

Central processor

The central processor processes the program currently stored in the computer's main memory. A part of the central processor fetches the instructions, one at a time in sequence, from main memory and executes them. The central processor keeps track of progress by storing various types of information in a set of memory cells known as registers. All memory cells are uniquely identified to allow information to be retrieved from where it has been stored. One register called the program counter keeps track of the next instruction to be executed. As the instruction is executed, the required data is fetched from the main memory and stored temporarily in registers called accumulators. The result of the calculation is built up in an accumulator prior to transferring it to the main memory. Other registers are used in conjunction with the accumulators to indicate such things as the fact that the result is negative.

In addition to the circuits that perform arithmetic, the central processor also contains control circuits to ensure that the actions taken are synchronized correctly. These circuits are based upon the oscillation of a quartz crystal, as used in quartz clocks and watches.

Computer memory

The memory of the computer consists of two types of microchips – Read Only Memory (ROM) and Random Access Memory (RAM). ROM is a permanent form of memory that contains program instructions in its circuits. The program may be built into the chip when it is manufactured or put later into a chip called a Programmable ROM (PROM) or Erasable PROM (EPROM). The programs held in ROMs or PROMs are permanent and cannot be changed. An EPROM is useful at the development stage of a PROM or ROM. A program can be tried out in the EPROM and if necessary erased, using ultraviolet light, and corrected until it has been perfected.

This is the method often used in research and development laboratories to design ROMs.

ROM is used for storing programs that need to be permanently incorporated into a computer, for example, to make the computer dedicated to a particular application such as reporting on and controlling the flow of oil in an oil refinery. A very common use for ROM chips is for storing the software that controls a microcomputer. Some microcomputers, such as the Commodore VIC, allow you to use a programming language as soon as you switch on because the necessary software is contained in a ROM chip. This avoids having to load this software into the computer's RAM from magnetic tape or disk.

All forms of ROM retain their contents when the computer is switched off. RAM, on the other hand, loses the information stored in it when the computer is switched off. It is therefore used as a short-term memory. RAM is the area of main memory used for holding programs typed in from the keyboard or read in from magnetic tape or disk. When a program is being run, data may need to be input from the keyboard or from magnetic tape or disk; this data will also be read into RAM.

Backing storage

Program and data can be stored off-line (on-line means there is a direct link to the computer; off-line means not currently linked to the computer) by recording them on magnetic tape or disk. Magnetic tape may be in cassette form or spooled, for reel-to-reel use. In either case, the characters, represented by their bit codes, are recorded across the *width* of the tape on a series of tracks. The zero and one bits are represented on the track by different states of magnetism. Information is recorded *sequentially*, that is, from beginning to end along the tape, and has to be accessed sequentially when it is read back into the computer. The device that both writes on and reads from the tape is known as a magnetic tape drive.

For some applications you may need to be able to 'jump' directly to the required information rather than travel in sequence to reach it. This can be done using a magnetic disk on a disk drive instead of tape. There are two types of disk – hard disks and floppy disks. The principles of storing information are the same for both types. Hard disks usually operate at faster speeds, have greater storage capacity, and are more expensive than floppy disks.

Floppy disks may have one surface (single sided) or two surfaces (double sided) for recording information. Some hard disks also have just two recording surfaces. However, hard disk units used with large computers generally have removable disk packs. Each disk pack has several disks, for example six, mounted on a common central shaft and separated by a space from each other. The outer surfaces of the disk pack are not used, giving ten recording surfaces for a six-disk pack. Hard disks may be totally enclosed in an air-tight box or may have a plastic cover to prevent particles of dust getting on to the disk surfaces. There is a read/write head for each recording surface. These can both write information on to the disk and read the information on it. The heads move in from the sides towards the centre and back while the disk revolves at a constant speed. Each recording surface of the disk is coated with a magnetically sensitive material. Information is recorded magnetically on concentric tracks.

A diagram of a floppy disk is shown in Figure 1.3. The disk is enclosed in a thin sleeve. When the disk is mounted in the disk drive, the disk rotates within the sleeve. The sleeve has a slot through which a read/write head can gain access to the surface of the disk. You can prevent information stored on the disk from being overwritten by use of the 'write protect' notch. Generally, you need to *uncover* the notch on eight-inch floppy disks to prevent them being overwritten, but *cover* the notch with foil to give write protection on five-and-a-quarter-inch disks.

As the read/write heads can be rapidly positioned while the disk is revolving, the head can in effect go direct to the information required. For this reason, disk drives are often called direct access devices.

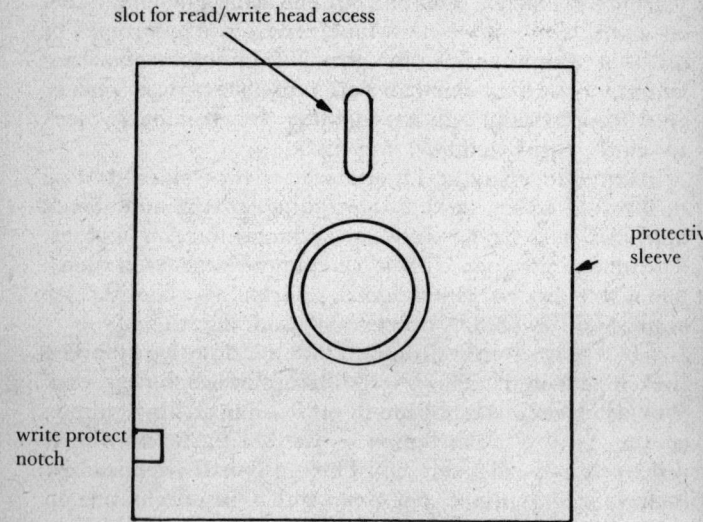

slot for read/write head access

protectiv
sleeve

write protect
notch

Figure 1.3   A floppy disk

Peripherals

Input devices – machines like keyboards, used to put information into the computer – and output devices such as those that produce information in a form people can understand, printers, for instance, both form part of a computer system and are called peripheral devices. There are many types of peripheral devices now available because as the use of computers has spread it has become economic to design special-purpose peripherals to suit a particular application.

One of the main means of input to a computer is via a keyboard. However, for certain applications it is possible to 'automate' the input. Perhaps one of the earliest commercial applications of automating the input of information was the use of Magnetic Ink Character Recognition (MICR) codes printed along the bottom of cheques. In this application the cheque number, account number and bank branch number are preprinted in a specially designed style of lettering. The ink used can be magnetized so that when the cheque is passed through an MICR reader all this preprinted information can be read automatically by the reader, thereby avoiding the need to key it into the computer system.

MICR requires the use of special ink and the style of lettering is difficult for a human to read easily. An alternative approach has been developed to overcome these limitations. The method involves Optical Character Recognition (OCR). OCR characters are much closer to normal typeface and are easily read by humans.

The OCR characters are input to a computer by scanning them with light-sensitive heads that 'read' each character. Providing there is sufficient contrast between the printed characters and the background, the heads can sense and decode the printing. This approach opens up the opportunity to have the computer produce printed output using OCR characters – telephone bills are an example you can look at. The output can be circulated, read by humans, and further entries made on the form. Finally, the completed form can be resubmitted to the computer system, when payment is made for example, to be read automatically without the need for keyboard entry.

Other ways of automatically reading information into the computer include bar codes and magnetic stripe. A lot of grocery items now have bar codes printed on their packaging. These codes appear as a collection of thin and thick black lines separated by spaces. When a light-sensitive pen is passed along the bar code, the pattern of light reflected by the bar code to a sensor in the head of the pen can be decoded by the bar code reader unit. Magnetic stripe is a similar idea, but the code is recorded on a short narrow stripe of magnetic material that looks similar to magnetic tape, usually incorporated as part of a price label. When the item is sold, a 'wand' (hand-held pen) is passed over the ticket and all the recorded details are read into what is known as a point of sale terminal (POS), which looks like a cash register, linked to a computer. These methods are useful in shops and similar situations because they are quicker and more accurate than having to enter the data by hand at a keyboard.

A similar light pen can also be used in conjunction with a VDU to select an item from an index of options displayed on its screen or to generate designs. Computer-aided design (CAD) is an important use of this feature and allows complex designs to be developed, readily changed and analysed. CAD techniques are used to develop the circuitry of micro-chips, among other things.

Another form of input is a joystick. A joystick is particularly useful for games that require the player to steer an object around the screen. Joysticks used with a microcomputer are similar to those used with television games and usually allow movement along two axes (up/down, left/right); some also have a pushbutton as a 'fire' control. The simplest joysticks simply 'switch on' the movement, say upwards, when you move the joystick in the up direction. You have no control over the speed of movement. The more elaborate joysticks have proportional controls, that is, the further the joystick is moved in any direction the faster the object on the screen moves in that direction.

The traditional output device associated with computers is the printer. Printers are manufactured in many styles and sizes. The main difference to note is the method of printing. The larger printers often have a cylindrical printing barrel which is the full width of the paper (up to 132 characters per line). There is a full width inked ribbon between the barrel and the paper. The barrel has a full set of characters (A to Z, etc.) around its circumference in *every* printing position along its length. The barrel revolves at high speed and at any instant a line of the same characters is opposite the printing hammers, which lie behind the paper. This means that if the letter is A, for example, an A can be printed anywhere along the line. A line of printing, therefore, is built up out of sequence, that is, not in a continuous movement from left to right, but is complete after one revolution of the barrel. The printer appears to print a line at a time, and for this reason it is called a line printer.

With the development of inexpensive microcomputers there is a corresponding need for cheap printers. One way of reducing the cost of printers is to have only one printing head, instead of a barrel, that moves along the paper. A common method of simplifying the printing head is to use a group, or what is known as a matrix, of needles. By activating the appropriate needles on the matrix, a pattern of dots is printed which corresponds to the required character. The size of the matrix may be different on different matrix printers. For example, a low-cost printer may use a seven- or six-dot matrix which does not allow descenders (printing below the line, as required for g, j, p, etc.) to be printed. Figure 1.4 shows a seven- by six-dot matrix for a £ character.

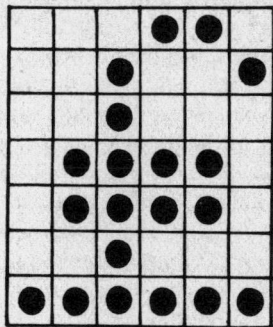

Figure 1.4   A 7 × 6 dot matrix for a £ character

Printers tend to be noisy, and attempts have been made to make them quiet. One approach is to put the printer in a sound-proof cabinet, but another approach, often used with dot matrix-type printers, is to use thermal paper. With this process, the needles gently burn the surface of the paper. Other methods of producing an image are to use an electro-static charge on specially treated paper, a process similar to the one used in photocopiers, or to direct jets of ink under the control of an electromagnetic field (ink-jet printers).

Another printer often found in offices is the daisywheel printer. Office work can require the production of high-quality output with speed and cost being of secondary importance. Daisywheel printers are usually slower than line printers and more expensive than matrix printers. The metal or plastic head of a daisywheel printer is similar to a head of a daisy flower, and each 'petal' has a character at its tip. In use, the daisywheel spins around in a circle as it moves across the paper, allowing any character to be printed in any position on the line. Another advantage of the daisywheel printer is that changing the typeface requires only replacing the daisy-wheel itself.

Continuous line drawings and diagrams can be produced on output devices, such as graph plotters, that use a pen. The computer controls the movement of the pen in two axes (or the pen in one and the paper in the other) and it can also lift the pen from the paper.

The main form of output with a microcomputer is the visual display unit (vDU). This unit consists of a cathode ray tube similar to a television set. In fact, with many personal computers you can use your ordinary television as the vDU. The information presented on the screen consists of approximately twenty-five lines of characters. The number of characters on a line varies from approximately twenty on some microcomputer systems up to approximately 132 on vDUs linked to large computers. Input/output units linked to computer systems are often called terminals. Graphics terminals are similar to vDUs except that instead of displaying just separate characters they can display continuous lines. Another method, used on several microcomputer systems, allows the individual 'dots' (called pixels) that make up the characters on a screen to be controlled by the program. This allows the screen to be used for graphic displays.

This section can only outline some of the very many developments in computer devices, and many of these may be difficult to visualize. However, once you have used a computer for a while you will be able to appreciate much more readily the uses and advantages of any other computer devices you may meet.

Communications

Early computers required that all data that needed to be input to the computer was delivered to a data preparation room, which was usually adjacent to the computer. With developments in computer communications, it is no longer necessary to locate terminals or other input/output devices near the computer.

A terminal can be linked to a computer system over ordinary telephone lines. To do this, the electronic (digital) signals to and from the computer equipment have to be converted into audio signals. The process of conversion into audio signals is called modulation and the conversion back into digital signals is called demodulation. The device that is connected between the telephone line and the computer to perform this task is called a modem (*mod*ulator–*dem*odulator). There has to be a modem at the computer end and at the terminal end of the telephone line.

The modem may be wired permanently into a telephone line, but alternatively it is possible to use a normal telephone receiver in conjunction with a small device called an acoustic coupler. An acoustic coupler has moulded rubber sockets forming a soundproof container into which the telephone handset is inserted. The output from the terminal's modem is a series of audio tones which is picked up by the telephone mouthpiece. The output from the computer's modem generates audio tones at the earpiece. A microphone at the earpiece feeds these tones into the modem. The advantage of an acoustic coupler is that no direct wiring is needed between the terminal and the computer; as telephone lines are used, the coupler can be used wherever there is a telephone.

An acoustic coupler, keyboard and printer can be built into a briefcase. This briefcase can then be connected via an ordinary telephone to any computer in the world that will accept the user. The user dials the computer's telephone number and the computer system responds by requesting that the user identifies him or herself by inputting an account number and password (further aspects of computer security are discussed in Chapter 7). When you communicate with a computer elsewhere in the world, the link may also involve the use of a satellite to transmit the signals for part of the distance.

POCKET
DATA ENTRY
TERMINAL

GPO 'PHONE

COMPUTER
SYSTEM

Figure 1.5   Pocket data entry terminal

It is possible to have a very compact terminal that communicates over the telephone (see Figure 1.5). This is a data entry terminal and it is about the size of a pocket calculator. During the course of a day, a salesman, say, can enter the orders he takes into the terminal's memory. When he gets home, he can plug the terminal into a telephone receiver mouthpiece, dial the computer's telephone number, and transmit all his orders into his company's main computer.

Another communications development is the linking together on one site of several microcomputers into a local area network (LAN). As well as being able to share common printers and disk units attached to the LAN, users can send messages to each other on their microcomputers through the network using special software. This facility is known as electronic mail.

Software

The computer devices, the hardware, do not by themselves allow a computer to function. The computer needs to follow instructions. These instructions, which form different types of programs to be entered into the computer's memory, are an example of software.

In order to use a computer system at all, one type of software, called the operating system, must already be present within the computer's memory. For example, a program devised to calculate the percentages gained by students in an examination cannot be read into the main memory – and therefore cannot be run – unless the computer is under the control of the operating system. The operating system may be built into ROM chips so that it is automatically present whenever the computer is switched on.

The purpose of the operating system is to provide the basic instructions to the central processor so that the various units which make up the computer system function as intended. In timesharing installations, where many terminal users share the central processor and peripheral facilities, the operating system supervises the input/output activity throughout the system and logs the use of the various terminals and peripherals. The operating system is able therefore to provide an analysis of the use of the computer system. In a timesharing system, the operating system needs also to have security facilities, as described in Chapter 7, to prevent unauthorized people from gaining access to the computer.

Programming a computer requires that a sequence of instructions is developed in the zeros and ones of the binary code understood by that particular machine; this is called machine code. Writing in binary is very tedious and exacting and can lead to many errors. To make the process easier, programs can be written in other codes called programming languages. The computer itself automatically converts the program from the language into machine code using translator programs which have to be in main storage during the translation process.

A range of languages is available to the programmer. Those that make use of mnemonic codes or binary digits are called low-level languages, while those that use English words and mathematical symbols are called high-level languages.

Low-level languages are translated into machine code by a program called an *assembler* on an instruction for instruction basis. At the same time, the assembler program can output information to indicate errors in the way the language has been used to write the program.

Instructions in high-level languages are usually equivalent to several machine code instructions. High-level languages can be translated into machine code by two types of program – *interpreters* or *compilers*.

Interpreters translate one instruction at a time when the program is being used. The interpreter waits for the computer to execute the translated instruction before going on to the next instruction. This means that any errors in the use of the original programming language (known as syntax errors) are not discovered until part way through a run.

A compiler translates the original program completely before it is executed. During this process of compilation any syntax errors that are found are listed on a screen or by a printer. The original program (the source program) is amended as many times as required until there are no syntax errors. The compiled (machine code) version is then retained for subsequent use. If the program needs to be corrected, the changes are made to the source program and the whole program is recompiled.

Most personal microcomputers use an interpreter (which is contained in a ROM) so that you can use the specified high-level language in an easy fashion.

Compilers are used in large-scale applications where the time taken to develop a satisfactory compiled program is offset by the advantages of having a compiled program for, say, daily use. In general, a compiled program, having been translated into machine code, runs faster than a program that has to be interpreted into machine code every time it is used.

There are many high-level languages in use. One of these, called BASIC (Beginners All-purpose Symbolic Instruction Code), was designed for teaching programming to beginners. It is available on most microcomputers and has been extended so that it can be used for many different applications. All of the programs in this book have been written in BASIC to run on a Commodore VIC microcomputer. Some examples of the programs modified to run on other popular microcomputers are given in Appendix B.

In writing programs for computers and running a computer system, there is often the need to perform certain tasks almost as a matter of routine. For example, there will be the need to regularly copy the information on a disk to another disk or tape to provide what is known as back-up copy in case the original disk becomes damaged or the information becomes altered by faulty hardware or software. There is a need to perform checks on the operation of the computer system – to test that all the memory cells in a RAM chip are retaining information correctly, for example. Programs that are written and used for these types of routine checks are called utilities as they help in the use of the system.

A group, or suite, of programs, written to suit the general needs of a certain class of user is called a package. Packages of these application programs are available for most standard business and commercial procedures, for example, stock control, accounting, mailing-lists. A software package usually contains options that allow the different users to customize it to their purposes. The advantages of packages to the user are that they save programming time and therefore costs.

2 Programming a Computer

Developing a program

Now that you know how computers work, you can start programming your own computer. Programming a computer is not difficult, but you will need lots of practice on your school's computer or on the microcomputer you have at home, if you are lucky enough to own a personal computer.

When developing a program, the first thing you have to do is to write down all you know about the application which you want to put on the computer:

the purpose of your program;
the data it will use;
any calculations to be carried out;
the way the results should be displayed (on the computer's screen or printer).

What you are doing during this first stage is analysing your requirements. The documentation produced at this stage will be added to as the program is developed.

As you learnt in Chapter 1, a computer program consists of a number of instructions giving all the steps needed to solve a particular problem. Some of these instructions will be executed by the computer one after the other, that is, in sequence. The order in which the instructions are executed in a sequence is always the same. In parts of your program, you may give an instruction which causes the computer to choose the next instruction or sequence of instructions to be executed, if the result of the first instruction is greater or less than a certain quantity, say. In this case, the computer has been programmed to make a decision based on the result of a test, and the program will branch to another part of that program.

An example

Say we need a program to handle two types of calculation. We want the program to *add* three numbers (entered from the keyboard) or *multiply* them. A simple program to do these calculations and display the result on the computer's screen is shown in Table 2.1; this has been written in BASIC.

Table 2.1 Simple BASIC program

```
10 PRINT "ENTER A FOR ADD"
15 PRINT "OR M FOR MULTIPLY"
20 INPUT C$
30 INPUT "X,Y,Z";X,Y,Z
40 IF C$="M" THEN 70
50 R=X+Y+Z
60 GOTO 80
70 R=X*Y*Z
80 PRINT
90 PRINT "RESULT =";R
100 PRINT "------------"
```

Let's go through this problem and then you can key it into the computer and run it (by typing RUN). RUN causes the computer to start executing the program, starting at the first instruction. Notice each instruction has a line number, 10, 15, 20, 30, and so on. These numbers have several different uses. First of all, the computer needs to know which is the next instruction in a sequence. Normally the computer will go to the next higher line number (unless the current instruction branches elsewhere). For example, in line 40 if c$ *is* equal to M then the computer is told to go to line 70. If c$ *is not* equal to M then the computer *does not* go to line 70 but instead carries on to the next line (line 50). We may want to change or add instructions to improve our program. An instruction can be changed by replacing the current instruction with the correct version and giving it the same line number. To allow instructions to be added, gaps are left in the line number sequence. For example, we can insert nine extra instructions (numbered 21 to 29) between instructions 20 and 30.

The first and second instructions in the program (lines 10 and 15) cause a message to be 'printed' on the screen to remind (prompt) us to enter the code A if the numbers are to be added or M if they are to be multiplied. Line 20 causes the computer to wait for your response to be input from the keyboard. To indicate that it has reached an INPUT instruction and is waiting for your response, the computer will automatically display a question mark on the screen. You need to press A or M followed by the RETURN key in response to this question mark. Line 20 also instructs the computer to store your response in a memory cell referred to as variable C$. The dollar sign ($) indicates that this variable is a *string variable*. When a computer is instructed to store a variable as a string variable it will accept any string of characters from the keyboard and store them exactly as received. The other type of variable is called a *numeric variable*. Numeric variable names do not end with a dollar sign and are chosen by the programmer to represent numeric values that can be manipulated mathematically. The rest of the variables in the program are of this type. It is a good idea to choose variable names to indicate what the variable represents. For example, in this program, C$ has been chosen to represent the type of calculation (that is, addition or multiplication) and R (see lines 50 and 70) to contain the result of the calculation. Although only single letters of the alphabet (followed by a $ sign for a string variable) have been used in the program, many microcomputers, including the Commodore VIC, allow you to choose variable names of several characters.

The prompt message "X, Y, Z" has been incorporated in the INPUT instruction in line 30. This message reminds you to enter three numbers that are to be given the variable names X, Y and Z. The INPUT instruction again causes a question mark to be printed immediately after the prompt. You then need to enter three numbers on the keyboard, separating them by commas, that is, 5,2,3. If you wanted to multiply these three numbers the screen output would appear as in Table 2.2. Because M has been entered from the keyboard at line 20, C$ contains M. Variables X, Y and Z are given the values 5, 2 and 3 respectively at line 30. When the computer executes line 40 it will jump to line 70 because C$ contains M. The instruction at line 70 multiplies X, Y and Z (* means multiply) and stores the result in memory cell R. Lines 80 to 100 produce the output. Line 80 simply prints a blank line on the screen to separate the following output from the input details. Line 90 prints the message "RESULT =" followed by the *value* of R, and this output is underlined by the instruction at line 100.

Table 2.2   Sample output

```
ENTER A FOR ADD
OR M FOR MULTIPLY
? M
X,Y,Z? 5,2,3

RESULT = 30
_____
```

The next calculation you may like to try (by entering RUN again) is an addition; the three numbers are 4, 6 and 15, giving a result of 25. In this case, the sequence of instructions executed will be lines 10, 15, 20, 30, 40, 50, 60, 80, 90, 100. The GOTO 80 instruction at line 60 is necessary because otherwise line 70 would be executed after line 50, giving a result of 360 (4 × 6 × 15). The GOTO instruction causes the program to branch to the line number specified in the instruction. In this case, line 80 is executed immediately after line 60 and line 70 is by-passed.

Flowcharting and testing

You can use the flowchart symbols given in Figure 2.1 to show the logic of programs in the form of diagrams. You can check the logic of your flowchart by going through it, following every path with suitable test data and check the coding of your program in a similar way. Figure 2.2 gives an actual example of a flowchart and is discussed on page 29.

The next stage is to key your program into the computer. You may make mistakes in your keying in or in the way you are using the programming language. These will be found by the BASIC interpreter or compiler (see Chapter 1, page 18). These mistakes are known as syntax errors and can be corrected using the method given in the user manual provided with your computer. Alternatively, you can key in the line again using the same line number so that the old version of the line is replaced (that is, overwritten in the main memory) by the new one. All syntax errors must be cleared before the program can be run with data.

Once the program has been proved correct, you should complete the documentation that you started during the analysis stage so as to provide a manual for the intended user. How comprehensive this needs to be will depend on the complexity of the program and who is going to use it. If you are writing the program for other people to use, then the users will need to understand what it can and cannot do and also how to run it (sample data should be provided).

The fizzy drinks problem

You've gone around the shops to check on the prices of various types of fizzy drink. The drinks come in different sized bottles and cans. You want to design and write a computer program that calculates the cost per litre of each type of drink.

Symbol	Use

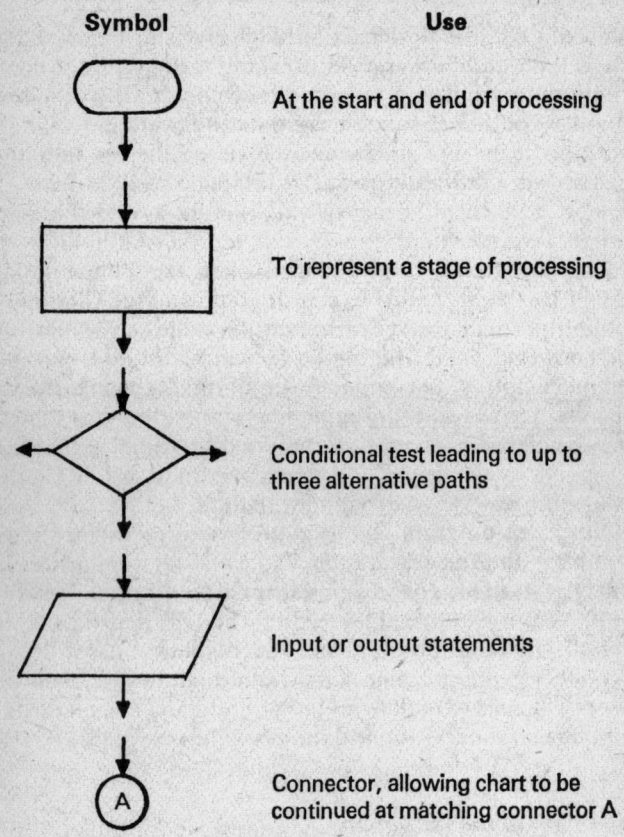

At the start and end of processing

To represent a stage of processing

Conditional test leading to up to three alternative paths

Input or output statements

Connector, allowing chart to be continued at matching connector A

Figure 2.1 Some flow chart symbols

Analysis of problem

The data consists of details for twelve types of fizzy drink (name, container size in millilitres (ml), and price in pence). All the data will be entered into the computer's memory and stored as lists of names with associated sizes and prices.

The cost per litre is found by dividing the price by the millilitre size and multiplying by 1000 to convert to litres (1 litre = 1000 ml). The answer should be rounded to the nearest penny.

The output has been designed for a 22-column screen (only 21 are used in Table 2.3). If your computer has more column positions, you can spread the table out across the screen. With only twenty-two columns you will need to abbreviate the names of the drinks. This restriction provides a useful exercise in programming, since any attempts to enter names which are too long will need to be rejected.

```
    FIZZY DRINK PRICES
    ------------------

    NAME SIZE PRICE COST/
         ML  PENCE LITRE
    ---- ---- ----- -----
    AAAA 9999   99    99  ⎫
    AAAA 9999   99    99  ⎬ up to 12 lines
      .    .    .     .   ⎪
      .    .    .     .   ⎭
      .    .    .     .
```

Table 2.3   Format of fizzy drinks computer output

Table 2.3 shows the headings and positions of the data within the table. This table shows the format, that is, the way the computer output is to be displayed on the screen. Positions of the alphabetic characters are indicated by an A and those of numeric digits by a 9. The dots indicate that there are several lines of similar format (12 maximum).

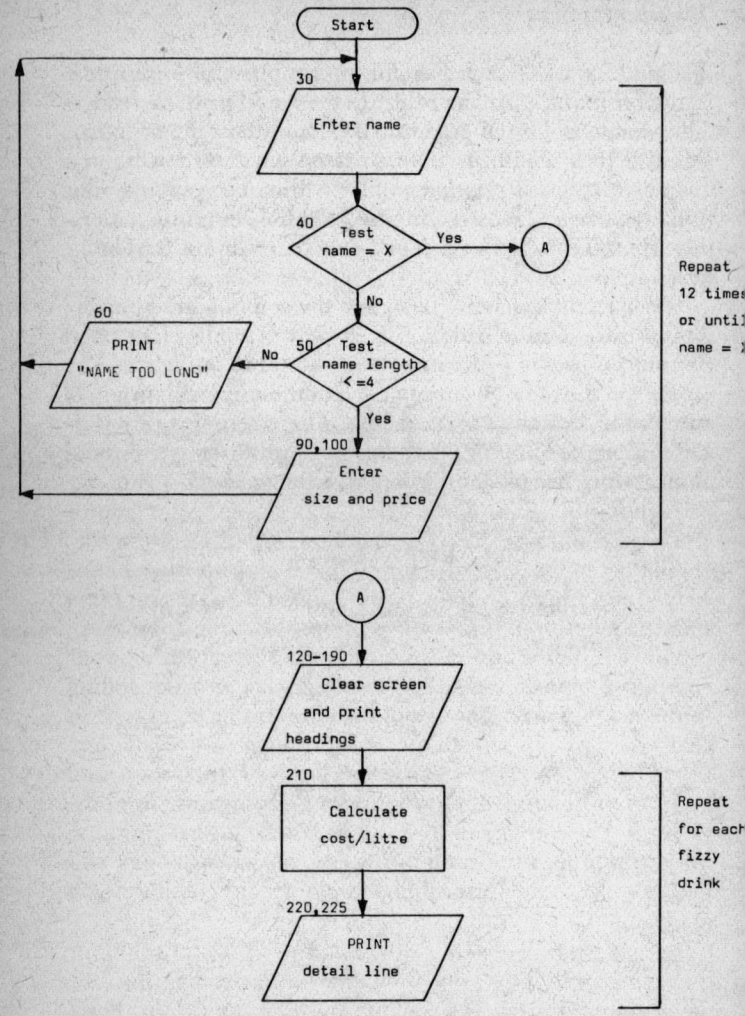

Figure 2.2 Flowchart for fizzy drinks problem

Flowchart

Figure 2.2 shows a flowchart for this problem; the program is shown in Table 2.4 (the box numbers in Figure 2.2 refer to line numbers in the program). The entry of the data is controlled by a variable K. This starts with a value of 1 and is increased by 1 after each set of fizzy drink data (name, size, price) has been entered and stored in the computer's memory. When K reaches a value of 13, the 'calculation' part of the program will be started. First the screen is cleared, then the cost per litre is calculated for each drink and a line showing the results of the calculation is displayed in the right-hand column, as shown in Table 2.3.

The program has been designed to process a maximum of 12 sets of data. The actual number to be processed is determined by the user. The end of the data to be processed is indicated by entering an x as the last name. This causes a branch to the calculation part of the program. After a name has been entered, and *not* found to be x, its length is tested. If the name has more than four characters, a message is displayed and the program loops back to line 30 so that another name can be keyed in.

You will find it useful to try out this program on your computer before studying the explanation of the BASIC coding in the next section. Then save the program on a cassette so that you can experiment by changing various things and seeing what the effect is. You can go back to the original program by loading it into the computer's memory from the cassette. The commands for saving and loading programs on cassettes are not the same for every computer, so you will need to refer to the instruction manual for the computer you are using.

Coding in BASIC

The BASIC instructions for this program are given in Table 2.4. Line 10 is a DIMENSION (DIM) instruction. This causes sufficient memory cells to be allocated for the three lists of names (N$), sizes (S) and prices (P). Line 20, together with

```
10 DIM N$(12),S(12),P(12)
20 FOR K=1 TO 12
30 INPUT "NAME";N$(K)
40 IF N$(K)="X" THEN 120
50 IF LEN(N$(K))<=4 THEN 90
60 PRINT "NAME TOO LONG (ENTER"
70 PRINT "4 CHARACTERS ONLY)"
80 GOTO 30
90 INPUT "SIZE";S(K)
100 INPUT "PRICE";P(K)
110 NEXT K
120 PRINT ""
130 PRINT "  FIZZY DRINK PRICES"
140 PRINT "  -------------------"
150 PRINT
160 PRINT "NAME SIZE PRICE COST/"
170 PRINT "     ML  PENCE LITRE"
180 PRINT "---- ---- ----- -----"
190 PRINT
200 FOR L=1 TO K-1
210 C=INT(P(L)/S(L)*1000+0.5)
220 PRINT N$(L);TAB(4);S(L);
225 PRINT TAB(11);P(L);TAB(16);C
230 NEXT L
```

Table 2.4 BASIC program for fizzy drinks problem

line 110, causes the instructions in between (lines 30 to 100) to be repeated up to 12 times. The variables have the counter name (K) in brackets so that the names, sizes and prices are stored in memory cells:

$$N\$(1),N\$(2),N\$(3) \ldots N\$(12) \qquad \text{(name list)}$$
$$S(1),S(2),S(3) \ldots S(12) \qquad \text{(size list)}$$
$$P(1),P(2),P(3) \ldots P(12) \qquad \text{(price list)}$$

The program will branch to line 120 from line 40 as soon as X has been entered for the name. All other names are tested in line 50. If the name is less than (<) or equal to (=) 4 characters in length, then it is acceptable and the program branches to line 90 to request the size to be entered. Otherwise, the message:

NAME TOO LONG (ENTER 4 CHARACTERS ONLY)

is displayed at lines 60 and 70 and the program branches back to line 30.

When all the data has been keyed in and stored as lists in the computer's memory, the screen is cleared by means of a clear screen character in the PRINT instruction at line 120. This will result in the cursor being positioned in the top left-hand corner of the screen, that is, the home position. The cursor is the name given to the symbol that is used to indicate where the next character will appear on the screen. The cursor symbol on the Commodore VIC is a blinking rectangle. You will need to check the format of the 'clear' instruction for your computer as it is not standard. Lines 130 to 180 output headings on the screen, appropriately underlined (lines 140 and 180), and separated by blank lines due to the PRINT instructions at lines 150 and 190.

The last part of the program (lines 200 to 230) performs the calculation for cost per litre (line 210) and outputs the results line (lines 220 and 225). The semi-colon (;) at the end of line 220 causes the output displayed by line 225 to appear on the screen on the same line as the output from line 220. Lines 200 to 230 form a FOR ... NEXT loop. The FOR instruction indicates the beginning of the loop and the NEXT instruction the end of the loop. The three instructions at lines 210 to 225 are repeated for values of L (for litre) starting at L = 1 to L = K − 1. This means they are repeated K − 1 times.

Line 210 divides (/) price by size to get price per millilitre and then multiplies by 1000 to get price per litre. Adding 0.5 to this result causes the integer (whole number) part of the result to be increased by 1 if the decimal part is 0.5 or greater. For example, if the result is 74.6, adding 0.5 will give 75.1. If the result is 74.3, adding 0.5 will give 74.8. The word INT, for integer, after the equals sign (=) causes the decimal part of the calculated result in brackets to be dropped. That is, 75.1 becomes 75 and 74.8 becomes 74. This has the effect of rounding the result to the nearest whole number, so that 74.6 pence becomes 75 pence and 74.3 pence becomes 74 pence.

Lines 220 and 225 contain TAB, which causes the next character to be output in the column position after the one shown in brackets after the TAB. Positive numbers are output with a space before them. This means that the names (N$) will be output starting in the first column, and the size (s) will be output starting in column 5 (which will contain a blank since it is positive) so that the first digit is output in column 6. Similarly, the first digits of the price (P) and the cost/litre (C) will appear in columns 13 and 18 respectively.

Testing the program

The test data for the program is shown in Table 2.5. Follow it through on your flowchart and program so that every box and instruction has been tested.

DATA

name	size(ml)	price (p)	cost/litre (expected result)
LIME	1000	45	45
LEMON			(NAME TOO LONG)
SODA	1500	73	49
PEAR	330	20	61

Table 2.5   Fizzy drinks test data

If you decide to make changes to your program, you must test it again with revised data if necessary. For example, you may like to write a similar program for your parents to use so that they can compare the prices of different products, such as washing-up liquids or paints. Finally, don't forget to document the programs so that they can easily be used by other people.

Further BASIC statements

The programs in the following chapters use some further BASIC statements. If you are not familiar with programming in BASIC, you should refer to the Glossary of BASIC in Appendix A and to the user manual provided with your computer. The programs in this book have been written to run on the Commodore VIC microcomputer. Appendix B contains hints for converting programs to run on some other popular microcomputers.

3 Communicating with Computers

Over the last few years a new technology has emerged which we call 'information technology' because it is about passing information between ourselves and computers. This technology involves developing improved ways in which we can communicate with computers and they with us and new methods by which a computer also can transfer information to another computer faster and more reliably. This has resulted in our being able to obtain up-to-date information from computers more quickly and effectively, and this is affecting business methods and the way we learn.

The man/machine interface

We can communicate with a computer in a number of different ways, as discussed in Chapter 1. In this section we will consider how suitably designed hardware and software can improve communications between the computer and ourselves, which is known as the man/machine interface.

Keyboards

Most computer keyboard designs are based on the standard typewriter key layout, sometimes known as QWERTY because of the positions of these keys as the first sequence in the top row of alphabetic keys. Additional keys are provided for special functions, such as delete, insert, etc. The numeric keys may be grouped in a keypad area like a calculator. This arrangement helps you to enter numeric data faster and more accurately, using only one hand, than when the numbers are along the top row of the keyboard. In commercial computing, the bulk of the data input to computers is numeric.

A keyboard that is going to be used for long periods of time needs to be designed so that it has features that allow the operator to enter data quickly and accurately; it must also be comfortable to use. The keyboard should be full size and have a positive key action so you can feel when the key has been depressed. It is often helpful to have the keyboard separate from the visual display so that the operator can move it to the most comfortable working position. A 'repeat key' facility is useful on some keys. When this facility is available, holding one of those keys down causes that character to be repeatedly input to the computer until the key is released. If you have this feature on your computer, you must remember not to leave your finger resting on the key while you think!

The main points that need to be considered in keyboard design, therefore, are keyboard layout (where the keys are positioned), keyboard position (separated from the visual display), positive action of keys, and special function keys or facilities (such as repeat). This, of course, is more important in companies where the keyboard may be used continuously by data entry operators or word processing operators (who are mainly concerned with entering and editing text). However, as you become more proficient at programming and use your microcomputer for more advanced applications, requiring longer programs and perhaps larger amounts of data, you will find that a well-designed keyboard makes using your computer much easier.

Prompts and help systems

Another aspect of the man/machine interface is concerned with how the computer communicates with *you*. This will depend on how the software has been written. In the first place, a 'friendly' operating system will be helpful so that the computer displays information to help you use the system and to tell you if you make a mistake.

For example, if you want to SAVE, that is, record, a program on a cassette tape from main memory using the VIC microcomputer, you type SAVE on the keyboard followed by the program name in quotes, for example:

SAVE "FIZZY DRINKS"

When you press the return key to signal the end of the line of input, a message will appear on the screen:

PRESS RECORD & PLAY ON TAPE

You then press the play and record buttons on the cassette tape recorder, having placed your cassette in the tape recorder first and positioned the tape ready to record. The VIC will record the name you have given the program (FIZZY DRINKS in this case) on the tape as a 'header' followed by the program. When it has finished it will display the message:

READY.

You should then VERIFY that the program has been saved correctly by rewinding the tape and typing:

VERIFY "FIZZY DRINKS"

The message that appears this time, when you press the return key, is:

PRESS PLAY ON TAPE

As soon as you press the play button on the recorder, the computer will read the information on the tape. If you have rewound too far, it will tell you the names of the programs it is finding in the headers so that you can reposition the tape if necessary. When it finds the program to be verified, it will display:

VERIFYING

and then compare the program recorded on the tape with the program in the computer's memory. If the two agree, the VIC will display the message:

OK

but if they do not, it will display:

? VERIFY ERROR

If you get a verify error, you will need to record and verify the program again.

Once the program has been successfully saved, you can switch off the computer and come back later, position your cassette in the recorder, and type in:

LOAD "FIZZY DRINKS"

and press return. The VIC will display the message:

PRESS PLAY ON TAPE

and after you have pressed the play button on the recorder, it will search through the cassette tape looking for a header containing the name FIZZY DRINKS (in the same way as when verifying). It will display the names of the programs found but will not load into main memory any other program except the one specified in the LOAD command.

This gives some idea of how an operating system can give helpful information in response to your operating commands (also known as system commands). When *you* design programs, you should keep the user in mind so that helpful messages appear at different stages. For example, your program may involve giving the user a choice from a list of options (called a menu). You can tell the user what the choices are and how to select the one he requires by displaying the menu on the screen.

Figure 3.1 is the main menu produced by a program called FAM-TEX (this is listed in Table 3.1, which is described later; see page 43). The screen displays a general heading with the options available to the user listed below it. The option is selected by keying in the appropriate number. For example, if you enter 100 to select FAMILY DATES, a second menu will be displayed, as shown in Figure 3.2, showing the types of dates (that is, BIRTHDAYS, ARRANGEMENTS, TERM DATES). You can

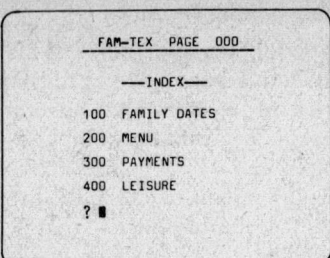

Figure 3.1 FAM-TEX menu

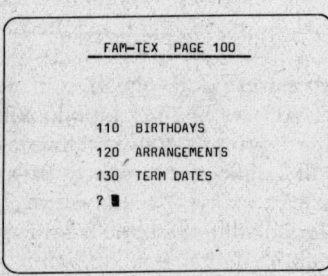

Figure 3.2 Page 100 showing FAMILY DATES

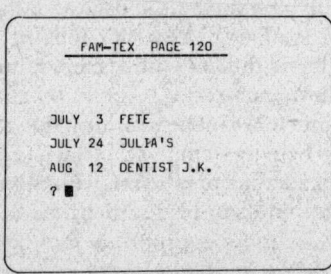

Figure 3.3 Page 120 showing ARRANGEMENTS

then make a further selection by entering the appropriate number, say 120 for ARRANGEMENTS. This will cause the information shown in Figure 3.3 to be displayed. Notice that this display is *not* a menu, as there are no numbers against the lines of information. You can return to the main menu (page 000) by entering 0.

When developing menus like this, the program should be written so that unacceptable entries (that is, options that do not exist) are rejected. In the example shown in Figure 3.1, if the user responds by entering 500, the main menu is displayed again. To keep the presentation of menus tidy on the screen and to prevent gradual scrolling (text moving up the screen) as the user responds with unacceptable inputs, the menu needs always to be displayed in the same screen location. This is achieved by using 'clear screen' commands each time before displaying the menu.

Alternatively, you could program the computer to ask questions which will prompt the user to put in an appropriate reply. For example, your program may process a number of sets of data from, say, a physics experiment. After processing each set of data you could cause the following message to be output:

ANY MORE DATA (Y/N)?

The user should reply Y or N as prompted by the message. A response of YES or NO should also be allowed for, as described in Chapter 7 (page 93), where the idea of 'user-friendly' software is developed further with respect to computer security. This will allow the user to respond by entering the first letter or the complete word, that is, Y or YES, N or NO.

Prompts and help systems are often used in programs specially written for business users who have no specialist experience of computers or programming.

Information through your television set

In the UK we can receive programmes in colour, if we have a colour television set, broadcast by the British Broadcasting Corporation (BBC) and by independent television companies. You may be using a television set also as a VDU with your home computer. Your display can be in monochrome (black and white) or colour, depending on the facilities available on your computer.

However, these are not the only uses that you can make of your television set. Videotex systems are available in many countries which transmit 'pages' of information (words and diagrams) from a remote computer either over telephone lines (using the viewdata system) or broadcast by a television station (using the teletext system).

Teletext

The two teletext systems available in the UK are:

Ceefax, offered by the BBC, and
Oracle, offered by the independent television companies.

These teletext systems broadcast information on news items, the weather, sports, entertainment, etc. to every television receiver. To view the information, your receiver will need to contain special circuitry called a teletext decoder. The teletext decoder may be incorporated in your television set or you can buy a separate adaptor which plugs into the aerial socket – you then plug the aerial into the adaptor. Alternatively, your microcomputer may have a teletext and viewdata decoder built in. You will also be provided with a small keypad similar to that on a calculator. This enables you to key in the numbers listed in the main index alongside each entry to reach the item of information you want.

Viewdata

The user of a viewdata system can communicate, via the telephone system, with the computer that holds the information. The system is also known as interactive videotex because the user communicates *directly* with the computer and the computer can respond *immediately* to the user. Companies can have their own in-house viewdata system on their computer. Such companies can then communicate information to their employees, who will be able to enter data, and access and process information held on the company's main computer files (the company data base), using adapted television sets as terminals.

A public viewdata system, called Prestel, is run by British Telecom (BT). This enables anyone who is a registered Prestel user and has a Prestel receiver – for example, an adapted television – to call up selected information on the television screen. This information is put on the Prestel system by Information Providers (IPS). These could be companies selling products, services or specialized information.

For example, a mail order company may hold its catalogue on Prestel. You could then browse through the menus by keying in the numbers listed on the index. If you select a product, you call up an order form on the screen, key in the details (perhaps your name, address and products selected) using your keypad, and then send the order via Prestel by pressing the appropriate button on your keypad.

Directories are available which contain details of the services offered by Prestel Information Providers. The charges vary according to the type of service provided. A mail order company may not charge you for looking at its pages of information; advertisers also supply free information. However, a company selling, say, information on share prices or foreign currency exchange rates is likely to make a charge for every page of information viewed; the price is displayed on the page. This sort of information is very valuable to business users such as banks and stockbrokers who require up-to-date information on financial matters.

Telesoftware

Another use of teletext and viewdata is for transmitting computer programs – telesoftware. This application will grow in importance as more organizations provide computer programs in this way.

Ceefax, Oracle and Prestel are being used for distributing software developed by educational organizations, to schools, colleges and home users. A suitably adapted microcomputer can be used to receive these programs directly into its main memory – the telesoftware is said to be 'downloaded' into the microcomputer. The user then can run the programs and also store them on cassette tapes for future use. Alternatively, teletext users can key the programs into their microcomputers as they are displayed on the TV screens.

Using Prestel

To use Prestel, your parents or your school would need to become registered as residential or business users of the Prestel system. Both types of user are charged for the time they are connected to the Prestel computer and for the telephone time used. In addition, business users pay a fixed quarterly charge.

A Prestel jack socket needs to be attached to your telephone line and a lead from your television set is plugged into this. To get through to the Prestel computer, you press a button on the keypad which automatically dials up Prestel. Your telephone is engaged while using Prestel and you cannot receive incoming calls during this period. At other times, the telephone can be used normally.

Pages of information on the Prestel system are linked together. If you don't know the number of the page you are looking for, you can look up a routing page which will point you to a 'lower-level' page. For example, you could look up Colleges of Higher Education to obtain a list of all colleges; this page can then point you to colleges in certain regions of the country. Finally, you may be pointed to a particular college and to pages of information for that college, such as the courses offered. However, if you know the number of the page required you can go directly to it.

Pages on the Prestel system are attractively displayed – words and diagrams can be coloured white, red, blue, green, yellow, cyan or magenta. These colours and black can also be set as background colours. The Prestel page has twenty-four rows of forty characters, any of which can be set to flash on and off to attract attention. Characters can also be set to double height for greater effect.

FAM-TEX

The FAM-TEX program which is shown in Table 3.1 (and see also Figures 3.1–3.3) demonstrates how a videotex system can be used to provide information. The FAM-TEX program allows you to set up your own family videotex system on your microcomputer.

The required pages to be displayed are written as a series of PRINT statements to suit your own requirements. The only limitation on the number of pages that can be created is the size of your computer's main memory.

Each page is given a three-digit number which forms the basis of the indexing system. The first digit indicates the main heading under which the page is classified. For example, you might assign all pages beginning with 1 to family dates (see Figure 3.1, page 38). The second digit indicates a sub-division within the main heading, e.g. 110 birthdays, 120 arrangements, etc. (Figure 3.2, page 38). The third digit is not used in FAM-TEX, but a three-digit system was chosen because three digits are commonly used in other systems. A possible arrangement of page numbers is shown in Figure 3.4. Notice that a list of main headings can be obtained by viewing page 000. The results of keying in 000, when the program listed in Table 3.1 is run, is shown in Figure 3.1.

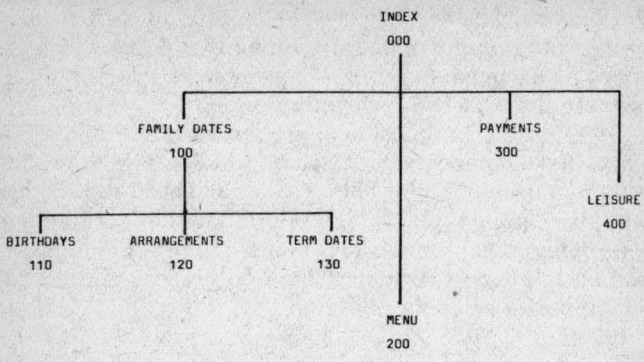

Figure 3.4   Structure of FAM-TEX pages

As we have said, the program is designed for you to set up your own pages of information together with your own headings. The program in Table 3.1 contains details of several pages. After we have explained the program instructions for using page 120, we will show you how to set up extra pages.

Line 10 is a REMark line giving the name of the program. There are REM statements in this program at the start of each section relating to a page. Line 20 initializes the page number (P$) to a three-character string of zeros prior to line 30 sending the computer to the routine in lines 500 to 599. This routine causes the main index (headings) to be displayed on the screen.

Within the main index routine (and all other page routines) there is a GOSUB to the subroutine at lines 100 to 150. This subroutine is used on each occasion to clear the screen of the previous display (line 110) and to print the current page number (P$) being displayed (line 120). Line 130 underlines the message printed at line 120, and line 140 produces a blank line to separate the heading from the rest of the page.

Having printed the page numbers of the main headings

Table 3.1   FAM-TEX program

```
10 REM FAM-TEX
20 P$="000"
30 GOTO 500
40 INPUT P$
50 IF LEN(P$)<>3 THEN 20
60 V=VAL(MID$(P$,1,1))
70 C=VAL(MID$(P$,2,1))
80 ON V GOTO 1000,2000,3000,4000,5000,20
90 GOTO 20
100 REM HEADING
110 PRINT"J":REM CLR SCREEN
120 PRINT"  FAM-TEX  PAGE ";P$
130 PRINT"--------------------"
140 PRINT
150 RETURN
500 REM INDEX
510 GOSUB 100
520 PRINT"    ---INDEX---"
530 PRINT
540 PRINT"100  FAMILY DATES"
550 PRINT"200  MENU"
560 PRINT"300  PAYMENTS"
570 PRINT"400  LEISURE"
580 PRINT"500  PRESENT LISTS"
590 PRINT
599 GOTO 40
1000 REM DATES
1010 ON C GOTO 1100,1200,1300,20
1020 GOSUB 100
1030 PRINT
1040 PRINT"110  BIRTHDAYS"
1050 PRINT"120  ARRANGEMENTS"
1060 PRINT"130  TERM DATES"
1090 PRINT
1099 GOTO 40
1100 REM BIRTHDAYS
1110 GOSUB 100
1120 PRINT"NOT SET UP"
1199 GOTO 40
1200 REM ARRANGEMENTS
1210 GOSUB 100
1220 PRINT
1230 PRINT"JULY  3  FETE"
1240 PRINT
1250 PRINT"JULY 24  JULIA'S"
1260 PRINT
1270 PRINT"AUG  12  DENTIST J.K"
1290 PRINT
1299 GOTO 40
1300 REM TERM DATES
```

```
1310 GOSUB 100
1320 PRINT"NOT SET UP"
1399 GOTO 40
2000 REM MENU
2010 GOSUB 100
2020 PRINT"NOT SET UP"
2099 GOTO 40
3000 REM PAYMENTS
3010 GOSUB 100
3020 PRINT"NOT SET UP"
3099 GOTO 40
4000 REM LEISURE
4010 GOSUB 100
4020 PRINT"NOT SET UP"
4099 GOTO 40
5000 REM PRESENT LISTS
5010 ON C GOTO 5100,5200,20
5020 GOSUB 100
5030 PRINT
5040 PRINT"510 GUY'S LIST"
5050 PRINT"520 MANDY'S LIST"
5060 PRINT
5070 GOTO 40
5100 REM GUY'S LIST
5110 GOSUB 100
5120 PRINT
5130 PRINT"DART BOARD"
5140 PRINT"FISHING ROD"
5150 PRINT"RADIO CONTROL CAR"
5160 PRINT"CB SET"
5170 PRINT
5199 GOTO 40
5200 REM MANDY'S LIST
5210 GOSUB 100
5220 PRINT
5230 PRINT"HAIR DRYER"
5240 PRINT"HORSE BLANKET"
5250 PRINT"GEOMETRY SET"
5260 PRINT"CASSETTE RECORDER"
5270 PRINT
5299 GOTO 40
```

using lines 540 to 580, line 599 sends the program back to line 40 to obtain a required page number from the keyboard. In every case, after displaying a page of information the program returns (with a GOTO 40 instruction) to line 40 to await the input of a further page number.

When a page number is entered it is stored in the *string*

variable P$. This allows line 50 to check that the string is three characters in length. If it is not, the program goes to line 20, sets P$ to 000 and then displays the main index. If the page number appears to be valid, line 60 extracts the first digit as variable v and line 70 the second digit as variable c. The values of these two variables are used later in the program to branch to the required set of print statements forming the desired page.

The value of v (1,2,3, etc.) is used in line 80 to branch to lines 1000,2000,3000,etc. This arrangement allows all page numbers in the hundreds (when v will be set equal to 1 at line 60) to be written using lines 1000 to 1999. Similarly, page numbers in the 200s are written using lines 2000 to 2999, and so on. The last number in the ON v GOTO sequence at line 80 should always be 20. This ensures that if a page number is entered that is higher than those currently available the resulting value of v will cause the program to branch to line 20 and reset the page number to 000. Similarly, line 90 ensures that the page number is set to 000 at line 20 if for any reason line 80 fails to operate.

Assuming a P$ string of, say, 120 was entered at line 40, then v will be set to 1 and line 80 takes the program to line 1000, as previously explained. At line 1010 branching now takes place, according to the value of c (if P$ = 120, then c = 2). Thus, in a similar way to line 80, branching will take place to 1100, 1200, 1300, etc. if c is equal to 1, 2 or 3 respectively. If c is greater than 3, control passes back to line 20 and the main index is displayed. If c equals zero (because P$ was set to 100) then no branching takes place and the program passes into lines 1020 to 1090. These lines display the index for the pages numbered 100.

We will now show you how to set up extra pages. Suppose that you want to set up lists of possible presents for your brother (Guy) and your sister (Mandy). You also decide that you want PRESENT LISTS to be a new main heading. This means that the page numbers must be in the 500s, as lower ones are already allocated. The index at page 500 can show that 510 is Guy's present list and 520 is Mandy's present list.

First we need to add PRESENT LISTS to the main index page by adding the following line to the program:

500 PRINT "500 PRESENT LISTS"

As v now may have a value of 5, line 80 needs to be extended as follows:

80 ON v GOTO 1000,2000,3000,4000,5000,20

Details of all new pages in the 500s will need to be written as PRINT statements within the line numbers 5000 to 5999. The first of these lines, 5000, can contain a suitable remark, for example:

5000 REM PRESENT LISTS

The next line required is an ON c GOTO branch that will take the program to the correct 500 page according to the second digit of the page number:

5010 ON c GOTO 5100,5200,20

When c equals zero (because page number 500 has been entered) the program will continue to the next line. The lines immediately following line 5010 therefore need to 'produce' page 500. Page 500 can be displayed by the program lines 5020 to 5070 shown in Table 3.1. Line 5020 produces the main heading by using the subroutine starting at line 100. The required contents of page 500 are written into PRINT statements at lines 5040 and 5050.

Pages 510 and 520 are set up in a similar manner, the only difference being the information contained in the PRINT statements. The program lines for page 510 could be lines 5100 to 5199. Page 520 could be lines 5200 to 5299.

You can see from the additional page routines given above that in general each should start with a REM and GOSUB 100 and end with GOTO 40. To emphasize this basic arrangement the original listing (Table 3.1) already contains these lines for several pages. To create your own version of these pages you just need to replace the print message "NOT SET UP" by the series of messages you would like to see on the screen.

Remember you don't have to stick with the original main headings; these are included to illustrate the idea. For FAM-TEX to be useful to your family you need to set up an index and series of pages that everyone will find interesting.

4 Playing Games

You can have fun using a computer to play games. At the same time you will learn how to use the computer's keyboard, how to load and run programs, and more about programming. We have included games for you to try on your computer and routines which you can use to develop your own ideas for games. These have been written to run on the Commodore vic microcomputer.

The games and routines have been designed to show you various possibilities. These will help you to understand how a computer can be used in an interactive way, where it is responding to the user's input. Read through the following list before trying out the games:

1 *Reaction timer* – uses the computer's ability to time your responses to randomly produced tests.
2 *Noughts and crosses, two players* – the computer is used to control the game and interprets the moves.
3 *Noughts and crosses, one player* – in this case the computer is the player's opponent, making moves of its own.
4 *Find the treasure* – the computer is used to set up and control the game and interprets the moves. It also acts as an opponent.
5 *Guess the number* – the computer sets up the game and acts as an opponent. It also displays its analysis of guesses to enable the player to improve his guesses.
6 *Scoreboard* – this uses the computer to keep the score for conventional games.
7 *Clock for two players* – the computer times each player's moves for games such as speed chess.

Reaction timer

The program for this game is shown in Table 4.1. The purpose of the program is to tell you how quickly you can press various keys on the computer's keyboard. The twenty-six letters of the alphabet, which are used for the test, are stored in the array x$ (dimensioned in line 10). The READ statement in line 20 takes each letter in turn (using the FOR . . . NEXT loop in lines 15 and 20) listed in the DATA statements (lines 25 and 27) and stores it in x$(1),x$(2) . . . x$(26),

Table 4.1   Reaction timer program

```
10 DIM X$(26)
15 FOR I=1 TO 26
20 READ X$(I):NEXT I
25 DATA A,B,C,D,E,F,G,H,I,J,K,L,M
27 DATA N,O,P,Q,R,S,T,U,V,W,X,Y,Z
30 PRINT"REACTION TIMER"
35 PRINT"--------------"
40 PRINT"THE COMPUTER WILL"
45 PRINT"DISPLAY ONE OF THE"
50 PRINT"LETTERS A TO Z"
55 PRINT"AND START A TIMER."
60 PRINT"YOU SHOULD PRESS THE"
65 PRINT"KEY FOR THAT LETTER"
70 PRINT"AS QUICKLY AS YOU CAN!"
75 PRINT
80 PRINT"NOW GET READY!"
85 PRINT"--------------"
90 PRINT
95 X=INT(RND(1)*26)+1
100 FOR I= 1 TO 2000:NEXT I
105 PRINT"PRESS KEY";" '";X$(X);"'"
110 A=TI
115 GET A$:IF A$<> X$(X) THEN 115
120 B=TI
125 T=INT((B-A)/60*10)/10
130 PRINT
135 PRINT"YOUR REACTION TIME WAS"
140 PRINT T;"SECONDS"
145 PRINT" ***********"
150 PRINT"ANOTHER GO(Y/N)?"
155 GET A$
160 IF A$="Y" THEN PRINT"":GOTO 80
165 IF A$="N" THEN END
170 GOTO 155
```

so that x$(1) then contains A, x$(2) contains B, and so on.

Lines 30 to 90 display instructions on the screen. Line 95 sets x to a value between 1 and 26 at random. Line 100 has been programmed to give a short time-delay before the selected letter x$(x) is displayed (line 105). As soon as it has displayed which key to press, line 110 stores the current value of the computer's internal timer TI in memory cell A.

The GET instruction (at line 115) waits for you to press a key on the keyboard and tests to make sure it is the correct key. If an incorrect key is pressed the program continues to wait at line 115. When the correct key has been pressed, the current value of TI is stored in B. Your reaction time is calculated in seconds at line 125 to one decimal place. You then can have another go by pressing Y, or stop by pressing N. If you press Y then the computer will clear the screen, by printing a 'clear screen' character in line 160, before telling you to get ready again (line 80).

Noughts and crosses

The program for this game is shown in Table 4.2. This is an example of a game where you POKE characters directly into a grid displayed on the screen. In this case, the grid has nine squares and the characters to be POKEd are the letters O and X, representing noughts and crosses. Line 5 changes the screen colour to light green and the 'writing' on the screen to black. Line 10 dimensions two arrays B and P; the purpose of these will be described later. Lines 15 to 25 display an underlined heading.

The grid and square numbers are displayed on the screen using simple PRINT statements (lines 30 to 70). The example shown is for the VIC-20 basic computer. The top left-most (HOME) position on the screen of this computer has the code 7680. The centre of each of the nine squares has been calculated as being a certain displacement (D) measured as

Table 4.2 Noughts and crosses program

```
5 POKE 36879,216:PRINT "■"
10 DIM B(9),P(9)
15 PRINT "⊃NOUGHTS & CROSSES"
20 PRINT "-----------------"
25 PRINT
30 PRINT "┌─┬─┬─┐"
35 PRINT "│1│2│3│"
40 PRINT "└─┴─┴─┘"
45 PRINT "│ │ │ │"
50 PRINT "│4│5│6│"
55 PRINT "└─┴─┴─┘"
60 PRINT "│ │ │ │"
65 PRINT "│7│8│9│"
70 PRINT "└─┴─┴─┘"
75 FOR I= 1 TO 9
80 READ D:P(I)=7680+D
85 DATA 89,92,95,155,158,161,221,224,227
90 B(I)=0:NEXT I
94 PRINT:PRINT:PRINT:PRINT
96 PRINT "PLAYER"
98 PRINT "ENTER SQUARE NUMBER"
100 GOSUB 1000
105 GOSUB 3000
110 GOSUB 2000
115 GOSUB 3000
120 GOTO 100
990 REM  PLAYER X
995 REM  --------
1000 POKE 8039,24:POKE 38759,0
1030 GOSUB 5010
1070 K=1:S=24
1080 RETURN
2000 POKE 8039,15
2030 GOSUB 5010
2070 K=-1:S=15
2080 RETURN
2090 REM TEST FOR WIN
2095 REM ------------
3000 POKE P(N),S
3010 B(N)=K
3020 FOR I=1 TO 3
3030 IF B(I)+B(I+3)+B(I+6)=K*3 THEN 3082
3040 IF B(3*I-2)+B(3*I-1)+B(3*I)=K*3 THEN 3082
3050 NEXT I
3060 IF B(1)+B(5)+B(9)=K*3 THEN 3082
3070 IF B(3)+B(5)+B(7)=K*3 THEN 3082
3080 GOTO 3092
3082 PRINT
3084 PRINT "PLAYER ";CHR$(S+64);" HAS WON!"
```

```
3086 END
3092 FOR I=1 TO 9:IF B(I)=0 THEN 3100
3093 NEXT I:PRINT"GAME DRAWN":END
3100 RETURN
5000 REM PLAYERS' MOVE
5010 GET A$:IF A$="" THEN 5010
5020 IF VAL(A$)=0 THEN 5010
5030 N=VAL(A$)
5040 IF B(N) <> 0 THEN 5010
5050 RETURN
```

the number of character positions from the HOME position,
where one line across the screen equals twenty-two characters. We therefore need to add $(4 \times 22) + 1$ to the HOME
position to reach the centre of the first square, which is on the
fifth line in the second character position; the displacement
D, in this case, is 89. All the displacements are listed in the
DATA statement (line 85) and stored as a list in memory cells
P(1) to P(9) (see lines 75 to 90). Another list B(1) to B(9) is set
to zero at the beginning of the game (line 90), and will be
used to indicate whether a square contains an X (represented
by storing a 1 in the B list) or an O (represented by a -1), as
shown later.

Player X always starts and enters the number of the square
he wants to put his X into. The POKE instruction in line 1000
puts an X (code 24) into screen position 8039, which is after
the word PLAYER on the screen, to prompt player X. When it
is player O's turn, he is prompted by the POKE instruction in
line 2000 which puts an O (code 15) on the screen after the
word PLAYER. Note that in line 1000, 38759 is the colour
memory location corresponding to screen position 8039.
POKE 38759,0 causes the character (X and O) POKEd to
position 8039 to appear in black. This actually needs to be set
only once in the program, so it could alternatively be put at
the beginning in line 5. Line 1030 branches to the PLAYERS'
MOVE subroutine (lines 5010 to 5050). This waits for a
number to be pressed and makes sure that it has not been
used before (line 5040). On returning from line 5050 to lines
1070 or 2070, K is set to 1 or -1 (to be subsequently stored in
the B array), and s to 24 or 15 (the character codes for X or O,
respectively).

Another subroutine, lines 3000 to 3100, is entered after either player's move, i.e. on returning from lines 1080 or 2080 to lines 105 or 115. Line 3000 POKES an x or o to the screen grid position N (which has the value 1 to 9) selected by the player. Note that N is obtained by converting the player's move, entered in line 5010, to a number using the VAL function in line 5030. Line 3010 stores the value in K (1 or −1) in B(N). Lines 3020 to 3050 test the result of the player's move. Three xs in the first column will result in B(1) + B(4) + B(7) in line 3030 equalling 3 (or −3 for three os) indicating a win for x (or o). The correct sign for 3 is obtained by multiplying by K (on the right-hand side of the equals sign in line 3030). The second and third columns are similarly tested, as a result of the FOR ... NEXT loop (lines 3020 to 3050). Horizontal rows are similarly tested for three xs or three os in line 3040. Lines 3060 and 3070 test the two diagonals for three xs and three os. If a winning line is found, the computer will display the message:

PLAYER X HAS WON! or PLAYER O HAS WON!

depending on which player has the winning line. Note that on the VIC, 64 has to be added to the character code value used in POKE statements to obtain the corresponding ASCII character code used with the CHR$ function (line 3084). If neither player obtains a winning line after all the squares have been used then the message:

GAME DRAWN

is displayed on the screen.

Noughts and crosses, one player

In the programs shown so far, the computer has not made any 'strategic' decisions. That is, we have not programmed the computer (acting as a player) to work out its own next 'move' according to the present state of play.

There are a number of problems involved in devising

programs for games that you can play against a computer, like noughts and crosses. First of all the computer cannot see the 'board' so we have to include instructions in our program to scan the grid before the computer can 'decide' on its next move. The decisions the computer makes have to be programmed based on 'winning' rules. However, it is not much fun playing against a computer that never allows you to win, so we will not program the computer to be an expert player.

This program starts as before (Table 4.2, lines 5 to 90). The following lines should be added to select whether the computer (PLAYER O) or the player (PLAYER X) should make the first move:

```
92 X = INT (RND(1)*2)+1
99 IF X = 2 THEN 110
```

Line 92 causes X to be set to 1 or 2 at random and line 99 gives the computer the first move if X = 2 by branching to line 110 that uses a new subroutine (lines 2000 to 2135) shown in Table 4.3. These lines replace lines 2000 to 2045 in Table 4.2. The computer uses this new subroutine to make the following strategic decisions:

1 If it is the first move, i.e. M is not equal to 1 at line 2005, the computer sets M equal to 1 (line 2007) and picks a number between 1 and 9 (line 2010) as its move. The move must be to an empty square, as tested in line 2015. When an empty square has been selected, a −1 is stored in its position in the B array (line 2020) before branching to line 2130.

2 For all other moves the program checks to see if the computer has a winning square to go to. H is set to −2 in line 2025 so that the program can test, over lines 2030 to 2055, whether there are already two os in a column, row or diagonal. The logic is similar to that used in lines 3020 to 3070 in Table 4.2. If it has a winning position, the appropriate grid number (N) is found over lines 2070 to 2080 *or* 2085 to 2095 *or* 2100 to 2110 *or* 2115 to 2125 depending on whether the *winning* position exists in a column, row or in one of the two diagonals. In each case the FOR . . . NEXT

Table 4.3 Computer's strategic moves subroutine

```
2000 POKE 8039,15
2005 IF M=1 THEN 2025
2007 M=1
2010 N=INT(RND(1)*9)+1
2015 IF B(N)<>0 THEN 2010
2020 B(N)=-1:GOTO 2130
2025 H=-2
2030 FOR I=1 TO 3
2035 IF B(I)+B(I+3)+B(I+6)=H THEN 2070
2040 IF B(3*I-2)+B(3*I-1)+B(3*I)=H THEN 2085
2045 NEXT I
2050 IF B(1)+B(5)+B(9)=H THEN 2100
2055 IF B(3)+B(5)+B(7)=H THEN 2115
2060 IF H=-2 THEN H=2:GOTO 2030
2065 GOTO 2010
2070 FOR N=I TO I+6 STEP 3
2075 IF B(N)=0 THEN 2130
2080 NEXT N
2085 FOR N=3*I-2  TO 3*I
2090 IF B(N)=0 THEN 2130
2095 NEXT N
2100 FOR N=1 TO 9 STEP 4
2105 IF B(N)=0 THEN 2130
2110 NEXT N
2115 FOR N=3 TO 7 STEP 2
2120 IF B(N)=0 THEN 2130
2125 NEXT N
2130 K=-1:S=15:GOSUB 3000
2135 RETURN
```

loop is left when the empty square is found. This value of N will be used in lines 3000 and 3010 in Table 4.2, as before, and causes the computer to win.

3 If there is no winning move, the computer checks to see if the other player has a winning square to go to. If this is the case, the computer makes the move that will block this square to prevent the other player from winning. The same part of the subroutine is used as for (2) above, but with H set to 2 in line 2060. That is, a line with two 1s stored in the B list is searched for, whereas a winning square for the computer is found in (2) above when a line has two −1s (that is, H = −2).

4 If there is no winning move for either the computer or the other player (x), then the computer makes a move as in (1) above.

Find the treasure

For some games you will want the computer to hide some objects for the players to find. For example, you could create a game for one or more players to find some treasure (hidden in a square as the number 1) with some mines (hidden as −1) that will eliminate the players if they land on those squares.

We can use the noughts and crosses grid and part of that program (Table 4.2) to show you how such a game could work. Three new subroutines – for hiding objects (Table 4.4), for testing the move (Table 4.5) and to sound an explosion (Table 4.6) – and the following changed and additional lines are required:

```
15 PRINT "⊐ FIND THE TREASURE"
92 GOSUB 805:z=o
99 IF z=24 THEN 110
105 GOSUB 305
107 IF z=39 THEN 125
109 IF z=15 THEN 100
115 GOSUB 305
120 IF z<>39 THEN 99
125 PRINT "THE COMPUTER WINS!":END
```

Table 4.4   Subroutine for hiding objects

```
800 REM HIDE OBJECTS
802 REM ------------
805 FOR I=1 TO 3
810 X=INT(RND(1)*9)+1
815 IF B(X) <> 0 THEN 810
817 IF I=1 THEN B(X)=1:GOTO 825
820 B(X)=-1
825 NEXT I
830 RETURN
```

The 'hide objects' subroutine puts a '1' (treasure) and two '−1s' (mines) in three randomly selected squares. This subroutine is entered from line 92, as shown above. Lines 805 to 825 (Table 4.4) form a loop that is executed three times to hide the three objects (treasure and two mines). Line 810 selects a square (1 to 9) at random. Line 815 tests if the square is currently empty and goes back to line 810 if it is not. Line 817 puts a 1 in the first empty square selected. Line 820 puts a −1 in the two other empty squares selected.

Table 4.5 Subroutine for testing moves

```
300 REM  TEST MOVE
302 REM  ----------
305 IF B(N)=0 THEN 330
306 PRINT "PLAYER ";CHR$(S+64)
310 IF B(N)=1 THEN 325
315 PRINT "HAS BEEN ELIMINATED!"
317 GOSUB 4010
320 Z=Z+S:GOTO 330
325 PRINT "HAS WON!              ":END
330 RETURN
```

The 'test move' subroutine (entered from lines 105 and 115 above) tests whether the square selected by the player contains a 1, in which case he has won, or a −1, which will cause him to be eliminated (the other player can continue until he wins or is eliminated). Line 305 (Table 4.5) tests whether the selected square is empty. If it is, the subroutine is left and the other player makes his move. Otherwise, the contents of the selected square B(N) is tested and a message is displayed for the player who has just made his move (306). If B(N) contains 1, the player wins (line 325). If B(N) contains −1, the player is eliminated (line 315) and the VIC generates the sound of an explosion (see Table 4.6, lines 4010 to 4080) as explained at the end of this section.

When *one* player has been eliminated, the other player can continue with the game. z is set to zero at the beginning of the game (new line 92). If player x is eliminated first, his character code s (i.e. 24) is added to zero (the current value of z) and then stored in z (line 320), so that z then contains 24. Similarly, if player o is eliminated first, z will be set to 15. When *both* players are eliminated, z will be set to 24+15, i.e. 39.

If player x has been eliminated (i.e. z = 24), the program jumps from line 99 to line 110 so as to allow player o always to move. Otherwise, the test move subroutine is entered at line 105. Similarly, if player o is eliminated (i.e. z=15), the program jumps from line 109 back to line 100 without entering the test move subroutine at line 115. If both players are eliminated (i.e. z=39), then line 107 branches to line 125 to display the message THE COMPUTER WINS! and the program stops. Line 120 jumps back to line 99 if one or both players have *not* been eliminated.

Line 5040 needs to be deleted as this was in Table 4.2 to ensure that an occupied square was not chosen, but in this game you can choose an occupied square containing a 1 or −1. Lines 3000 to 3100 are not required for this game and should also be deleted.

Table 4.6 Explosion subroutine

```
4000 REM EXPLOSION
4010 POKE 36877,140
4020 FOR L=15 TO 0 STEP -1
4030 POKE 36878,L
4040 FOR D=1 TO 300
4050 NEXT D
4060 NEXT L
4070 POKE 36877,0
4080 RETURN
```

The explosion subroutine (Table 4.6) generates a sudden noise which gradually dies away. Line 4010 produces the initial noise by selecting a particular sound (140) and POKEing it to the noise generator at memory location 36877. Lines 4020 to 4060 form a FOR . . . NEXT loop that progressively reduces the value of L from 15 to 0. Line 4030 within the loop sets the volume control (memory location 36878) to level L. Lines 4040 and 4050 form a time-delay to control the total time taken for the sound to die down to zero. Line 4070 switches off the noise generator.

Table 4.7 Guess the number program

```
5 POKE 36879,216:PRINT"∎"
10 PRINT ":∃THE COMPUTER WILL"
15 PRINT "THINK OF A 3-DIGIT"
20 PRINT "NUMBER FOR YOU"
25 PRINT "TO GUESS."
30 PRINT "IN RESPONSE TO EACH ?"
35 PRINT "ENTER 3 DIGITS."
45 PRINT "THE COMPUTER WILL"
50 PRINT "DISPLAY A ▨ ▆ FOR EACH"
55 PRINT "CORRECT DIGIT WHICH"
60 PRINT "IS IN THE CORRECT"
65 PRINT "POSITION AND A ▨"
70 PRINT "FOR EACH CORRECT"
75 PRINT "DIGIT WHICH IS IN"
80 PRINT "THE WRONG POSITION."
85 PRINT "THE ▨ ▆ & ▨ CHARACTERS"
90 PRINT "ONLY SHOW THE NUMBER"
95 PRINT "OF DIGITS CORRECT NOT"
100 PRINT "THE CORRECT POSITIONS."
110 PRINT "PRESS ANY KEY TO"
111 PRINT "CONTINUE"
112 GET A$:IF A$="" THEN 112
120 Z$=MID$(STR$(INT(RND(1)*889)+111),2)
200 PRINT ":∃ENTER YOUR GUESS"
210 PRINT "AS 3 DIGITS IN"
220 PRINT "RESPONSE TO EACH ?"
230 PRINT "------------------"
250 C=0:W=0
260 INPUT X$
290 FORI=1TO3:S(I)=0:NEXTI
295 FOR I=1 TO 3
300 IF MID$(X$,I,1)=MID$(Z$,I,1) THEN 335
305 FOR J=1 TO 3
310 IF MID$(X$,J,1)<>MID$(Z$,I,1) THEN 325
315 IF S(J)=1 THEN 325
317 S(J)=1
320 W=W+1:GOTO 340
325 NEXT J
330 GOTO 340
335 C=C+1
337 S(I)=1
340 NEXT I
350 PRINT ":∃";TAB(8);
355 IF C=0 THEN 365
360 FOR I=1 TO C:PRINT "▨ ▆ ";:NEXT I
365 IF W=0 THEN 380
370 FOR I=1 TO W:PRINT "▨ ";:NEXT I
380 PRINT:PRINT
390 IF C < 3 THEN 250
400 PRINT "CONGRATULATIONS"
```

```
410 PRINT "YOU'VE GUESSED IT!"
415 PRINT "-------------------"
420 PRINT:INPUT "ANOTHER GO (Y/N)";Y$
430 IF Y$ <> "Y" THEN 470
440 INPUT "INSTRUCTIONS(Y/N)";Q$
450 IF Q$="Y" THEN 10
460 GOTO 120
470 END
```

Guess the number

Table 4.7 shows a program in which the computer 'thinks' of a three-digit number (any number between 111 and 999) for you to guess. Lines 10 to 111 display the instructions on how to play the game on the screen. Note that lines 50 and 85 contain special characters called reverse video characters to reverse the background and foreground colours, in order to change a space into a solid square. The reverse video mode is turned on by pressing the RVS ON key (shown as ▨) and turned off by pressing the RVS OFF key (shown as ▪). Line 112 waits for you to press any key when you are ready to play. Line 120 generates a three-digit number at random, changes this to a string variable (using the STR$ function), and then eliminates the sign character by the use of MID$ starting at the second character of the string. The three digits of the number are stored as three characters in the string Z$.

Lines 200 to 230 ask you to enter your guess. Line 250 sets the number of digits in the correct position (c) and the number that are correct but in the wrong position (w) to zero.

Every time you enter your guess (as a three-digit number) in response to the INPUT statement in line 260, the computer will analyse your guess and tell you how well you have done. Line 290 puts zeros in the s array; this is used later in the program to record the existence of a match by putting a 1 in that position of the s array. Line 300 compares each of the digits in your number with the one in the *corresponding* position of the number chosen by the computer. If a matching digit is found, the program branches to line 335, where the value of c is increased by one, and puts a 1 in the s array (line 337) to indicate a match has been found in this position.

If the corresponding digits don't match, the three digits in your number are compared in turn with *one* digit of the number chosen by the computer (line 310) to find if any of your digits match. If a matching digit is found, that position is tested in the s array to see if this match has been found previously (line 315), in which case it is ignored by branching to line 325. Otherwise, a match in this position is recorded in the s array (line 317) and the value of w is increased by one (line 320).

Lines 350 to 370 display the number of correct digits in the correct positions (as a number of ∎), at line 360, and in the wrong positions (as a number of ▓ symbols) at line 370. This helps you to think how to improve your guess. When you have guessed the correct number (that is, c=3, as tested at line 390), the computer will congratulate you (lines 400 to 415) and ask whether you would like to have another go (line 420) and if so whether you would like to see the instructions again (line 440).

Scoreboard

With many games, such as scrabble or snooker, you need to keep each player's score as individual running totals. Each score shown is the sum of that player's scores so far in the game.

The program shown in Table 4.8 displays a scoreboard on the computer's screen for up to four players. You are asked to enter the number of players in line 40. If the number entered is greater than four, a warning message is displayed and you are sent back at line 50 to line 40. Line 60 dimensions the arrays to be used, P$ (for player's name) and s (for the score) according to the number of players entered, that is, the value of N.

Lines 70 to 110 form a loop to allow the names of the players to be entered from the keyboard (line 90). If the

Table 4.8 Scoreboard program

```
10 C$="▒░░░░░░░░░░░░░░░░░░░░░░░░░░░░░░"
20 POKE 36879,216
30 PRINT "▓"
40 INPUT "NO. OF PLAYERS";N
45 IF N<5 THEN 60
50 PRINT "NOT MORE THAN FOUR":PRINT:GOTO 40
60 DIM P$(N),S(N)
70 FOR I=1 TO N
80 PRINT "NAME OF PLAYER";I
90 INPUT P$(I)
95 IF LEN(P$(I))<13 THEN 110
100 PRINT "NAME LENGTH NOT MORE"
103 PRINT "THAN 12 LETTERS"
105 PRINT:GOTO 80
110 NEXT I
120 PRINT "▛▀                    ▜"
130 FOR I=1 TO N
140 FOR J=1 TO 3
150 PRINT "▌ ▐";TAB(14);"▌ ▐";TAB(20);"▌ ▐"
160 NEXT J
170 PRINT "▙                    ▟"
180 NEXT I
190 FOR I=1 TO N
200 PRINT LEFT$(C$,4*I-1);"▐";P$(I)
210 NEXT I
220 FOR I=1 TO N
230 PRINT LEFT$(C$,19);"SCORE FOR PLAYER";I
240 PRINT:PRINT"        ":PRINT"▔▔"
250 INPUT S
260 S(I)=S(I)+S
270 PRINT LEFT$(C$,4*I-1);TAB(15);S(I)
280 NEXT I
290 GOTO 220
```

length of the name entered is greater than twelve characters it is not accepted (line 95), a warning message is displayed (lines 100 and 103) and the user is sent back at line 105 to line 80.

The players' names and scores are boxed in reverse blue video to give a clear display (lines 120 to 180). Line 200 takes the cursor to the correct position on the screen for displaying the players' names inside the boxes, by selecting part of the C$ string in line 10. This moves the cursor to the HOME position and then an appropriate number of lines down. Similarly, line 230 takes the cursor down to the nineteenth row on the screen to display the message:

SCORE FOR PLAYER 1, etc.

Line 240 is used to delete the previous player's score from the screen by overwriting it with spaces, and to re-position the cursor (using two 'cursor up' control characters in the third PRINT statement in line 240) ready to receive the next score. The new score is entered in response to the INPUT statement in line 250. Line 260 adds the player's latest score to his total score before displaying this in the box next to his name (line 270).

Clock for two players

The program shown in Table 4.9 can be used to time two players' moves for speed chess, speed draughts, and so on. You enter the time-limit for the players in response to the INPUT statement at line 20; the time-limit is then in location TL. Then enter W or B to say whether white or black is to start (line 30). Line 40 is used to calculate N, which will be either 1, if W (character code 87) has been entered, or 0 if B (character code 66) has been entered. The values of N are used later in the program for adding the elapsed time to the appropriate memory cells P(0) or P(1) for black or white, respectively.

The current value of the internal timer (TI) is stored in memory cell A (line 60). Lines 70 to 130 form a continuous loop which is left either when a player presses any key on the keyboard (line 130) or the time-limit (set in line 20) is exceeded in line 120. This looping causes the value of D (for 'duration') in line 70 to be continuously revised as the value of TI increases. The initial value of D on entering this loop is P(N). This is because initially A is set equal to TI at line 60, and hence TI-A in line 70 is zero at this stage.

The contents of D need to be displayed on the screen in minutes and seconds. The minutes part (M) is calculated in line 80 by dividing D by the constant 3600 and using INT to

Table 4.9 Clock for two players program

```
20 INPUT ":TIME LIMIT IN MINS";TL:PRINT
30 INPUT"STARTING COLOUR(W/B)";C$
40 N=INT(ASC(C$)/87)
50 PRINT ":";TAB(4);"WHITE";TAB(14);"BLACK"
60 A=TI
70 D=P(N)+TI-A
80 M=INT(D/3600)
90 S=INT(D/60)-60*M
100 T$=MID$(STR$(M),2)+":"+MID$(STR$(S),2)+" "
110 PRINT "XXX";TAB(14-N*10);T$
120 IF D>TL*3600 THEN 170
130 GET A$:IF A$="" THEN 70
140 P(N)=D
150 N=1-N
160 GOTO 60
170 IF N=1 THEN 190
180 PRINT "XX";TAB(5);"WHITE WINS!":END
190 PRINT "XX";TAB(5);"BLACK WINS!":END
```

drop the decimal places, which form the remainder. Similarly, line 90 calculates the remainder as seconds (s) to allow the elapsed time for the player to be set up in the string T$ (line 100) for displaying on the screen (line 110), as shown in Figure 4.1. Line 100 actually takes four strings – the minutes without the plus sign, a colon, the seconds without the plus sign and a space – and joins these together as one string using the + signs.

When the loop (lines 70 to 130) is left because a player has pressed a key (at line 130) the duration (D) is stored in P(N) at

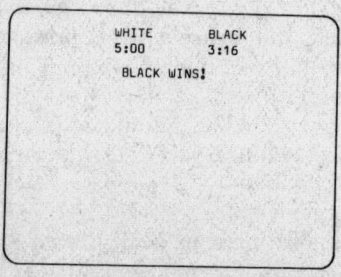

Figure 4.1 Output from clock program

line 140 and N takes the alternate value, for the other player, at line 150 (that is, if N was 1, N becomes 0, and if N was 0, it becomes 1). The program returns from line 160 to line 60 where A is set to the current value of TI and the *current* player's elapsed time P(N) is stored in D in line 70.

When either player exceeds the time-limit (as tested in line 120), a branch is made to line 170 to determine the winner. If N is currently 1, this indicates that the time ran out for the white player and black wins (line 190). Similarly, if N is 0, white wins (line 180).

An example of the display, for a time-limit of five minutes, is shown in Figure 4.1.

5 Drawing Charts and Pictures

This chapter includes four programs that make use of your computer's ability to display 'pictures' on the screen. You can use pictures in many ways – to present information more clearly, to make games more interesting and, by using the RND function (random generator) in BASIC, to produce unexpected patterns of movement, colour, and so on.

You will already have seen from Chapter 4 that you can design a picture, such as the lines for noughts and crosses, by printing a pattern of graphics characters on the screen. You also POKEd characters directly to particular screen locations. The programs in this chapter use these ideas together with the manipulation of strings, such as the use of MID$ in the CLOCK program (page 65) to produce further effects.

Here is a summary of the four programs:

1 *Bar chart* – data entered for the seven days of the week, for example rainfall, is presented as bar charts. The program demonstrates the idea of scaling any data to make sure it fits on the screen.

2 *Face* – a face made from graphics characters alternately sulks and smiles as a result of POKEing the mouth characters.

3 *Caterpillar* – a caterpiller crawls slowly across the screen to illustrate simple animation.

4 *Patterns* – a symmetrical mosaic pattern is produced using colours chosen at random by the computer. The program continues indefinitely, producing many variations.

Bar chart

This program draws a horizontal bar chart for each of the seven days of the week for data that is entered from the keyboard (see Figure 5.1). The data might be the results of any investigation you have done related to days of the week, such as the number of hours of television you watched, how much pocket money you spent, and so on.

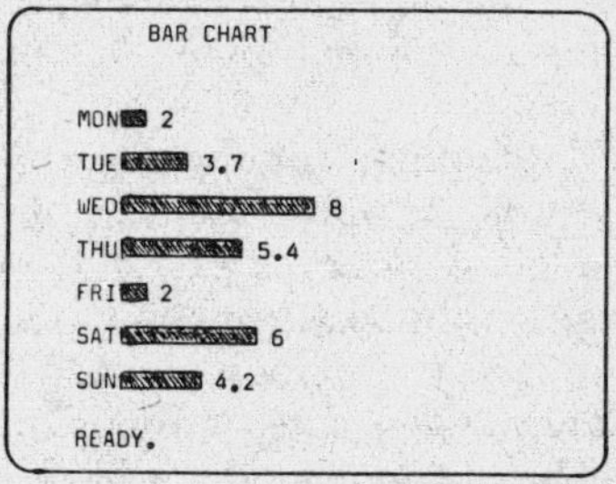

BAR CHART

MON 2
TUE 3.7
WED 8
THU 5.4
FRI 2
SAT 6
SUN 4.2

READY.

Figure 5.1 Output from bar chart program

The program is given in Table 5.1. Line 10 sets up the string D$; D$ contains all the days of the week within the one string. The subroutine at line 300 selects from this string the

Table 5.1 Bar chart program

```
10 D$="MONTUEWEDTHUFRISATSUN"
20 B$="▨                    ▓"
100 FOR D=1 TO 7
110 GOSUB 300
120 PRINT "ENTER VALUE FOR ";T$
130 INPUT N(D)
135 IF MAX<N(D)THEN MAX=N(D)
140 NEXT D
200 PRINT "🗋     BAR CHART"
210 PRINT "▓▓▓▓"
220 FOR D=1 TO 7
230 GOSUB 300
240 L=INT(15*N(D)/MAX+0.5)
250 PRINT T$;LEFT$(B$,L);"▓";N(D)
260 PRINT
270 NEXT D
280 END
300 T$=MID$(D$,D*3-2,3)
310 RETURN
```

required three characters depending on the value of D and stores these in the string T$. If D = 1 then D*3-2 has the value 1, so that the first three characters, MON, are selected. If D = 2 then D*3-2 has the value 4, so that the second three characters, TUE, are selected, since the selection starts with the fourth character of the string D$.

A second string is set up in line 20 (B$) to contain a line of 15 space characters in reverse video. If B$ were printed on the screen, a horizontal bar 15 characters wide would appear. Fifteen characters have been chosen as the maximum length of bar to be plotted.

Lines 100 to 140 form the input phase where the values to be drawn as bars on the screen are entered in turn into the array N(D) for each of the seven days of the week. Line 110 causes T$ to contain the required day of the week for each value of D, for use in the prompt line at 120. Line 135 makes sure that the largest value entered also is transferred to the variable MAX. The maximum value will be needed later to scale the data over the range 0 to 15 characters.

The output phase begins at line 200. Lines 200 and 210 clear the screen, print the main heading and move the cursor down three lines. The results for each day are then produced within the loop 220 to 270. Line 240 calculates the length of the line (L) to be displayed (the 0.5 ensures that L is correctly rounded). Line 250 prints the day (T$) and L characters of the bar string B$. As the bar is in 'reverse character', a 'reverse off' character is needed before printing the actual values at the end of the bar.

You may wish to change the character plotted as a bar to something more appropriate for the data, for example, plot £ characters for spending. To do this you need only alter B$ in line 20 so that it contains a string of your chosen symbol. The number of characters in string B$ must be the maximum length of bar you wish to plot. If you have a wider screen you may wish to go up to, say, 30 characters. Whatever number you choose must also replace the 15 in line 240. Remember that if you try to plot bars that are too wide for your screen, the display will 'wrap round', that is, run over, to the next line and cause you to think the program is completely incorrect as the display may just look a mess.

Face

This program produces a face on the screen by POKEing graphics character codes read from data statements. The mouth is made up from two characters; one set of these characters forms a smile and another set a sulk (see Figure 5.2). Once the face is drawn, only the characters for the mouth are changed to provide animation.

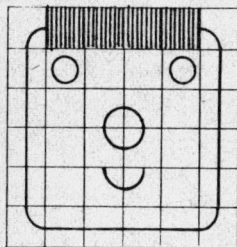 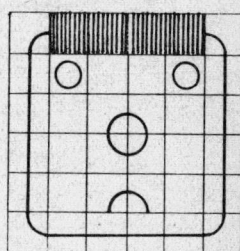

Figure 5.2 Animated face

The program is given in Table 5.2. Line 5 clears the screen. Line 10 sets SM to 7680 (the 'home position') and CM to 38400 (the corresponding colour code memory location) for the VIC. Lines 20 and 30 move the cursor down eight lines (of twenty-two characters) and move it along eight places. The characters required for the face are in data lines 200 to 250. As the completed face consists of a block of six characters by six, the data lines are written in an equivalent form of six lines of six character values.

The data lines are read within the loop over lines 40 to 100. The loop counts I and J are used to calculate the screen position and colour position to be POKEd while the data value read is the value POKEd (the data values are those required for the VIC screen code characters). On leaving this loop, the face will have been drawn on the screen, minus its mouth. The two character values to be POKEd to form the mouth are

Table 5.2   Animated face program

```
5 PRINT ""
10 SM=7680:CM=38400
20 S=SM+22*8+8
30 C=CM+22*8+8
40 FOR I=0 TO 5
50 FOR J=0 TO 5
60 READ X
70 POKE S+22*I+J,X
80 POKE C+22*I+J,6
90 NEXT J
100 NEXT I
110 X=74:Y=75:CL=6
115 XA=85:YA=73
120 FOR I=1 TO 10
130 POKE S+22*4+2,X
140 POKE C+22*4+2,CL
150 POKE S+22*4+3,Y
160 POKE C+22*4+3,CL
170 FOR D=1 TO 1000:NEXT D
180 XB=X:X=XA:XA=XB
185 YB=Y:Y=YA:YA=YB
190 NEXT I
200 DATA 85,102,102,102,102,73
210 DATA 93,87,96,96,87,93
220 DATA 93,96,85,73,96,93
230 DATA 93,96,74,75,96,93
240 DATA 93,96,96,96,96,93
250 DATA 74,64,64,64,64,75
```

assigned to x and y in line 110, together with the colour value. The two alternative values to be POKEd are assigned in line 115 to XA and YA.

Lines 120 to 190 form a loop to POKE the two alternative mouths to the screen ten times to illustrate simple animation. After POKEing the initial values of x and y, there is a delay built in at line 170 to slow down the change from one mouth to the other. Lines 180 and 190 switch the values of x and XA, and y and YA, so that when the loop repeats, the alternative mouth is POKEd to the screen.

You could try making different faces by altering the data lines to suit the graphics characters you have. A more detailed face could be drawn if you increase the number of characters from six by six, and then you could try getting your face to wink an eye or have its hair stand on end.

Caterpillar

This program has been written to illustrate how movement across the screen can be introduced into a picture. In this case, a small caterpillar crawls slowly across the screen.

The principle of animated movement is to have statements in the program which not only reposition the item you want to move but also erase the previous position. Usually, erasure of a previous position is done by printing a space in place of the character to be erased. In complicated pictures, however, when a moving item passes in front of other lines, the program logic has to test for and return the original character.

Table 5.3 Caterpillar program

```
10 L$(1)="<▓▓▓o"
20 L$(2)="<▓▓▓o"
30 S$="                    "
40 K=2:X=-1:Z=1
110 FOR I=1 TO 17
112 FOR L=1 TO 2
115 PRINT"▓▓▓▓▓▓▓"
120 PRINT LEFT$(S$,I);L$(K)
125 FOR D=1 TO 500:NEXT D
130 Z=Z*X
140 K=K+Z
145 NEXT L
150 NEXT I
```

The program is given in Table 5.3. Lines 10, 20 and 30 assign the three string variables that are used for the animation. To make the caterpillar appear to crawl, two strings are used to depict the caterpillar. L$(1) represents the caterpillar 'stretching' and L$(2) represents the caterpillar 'contracted'. The third string, S$, is a line of spaces used for positioning the caterpillar across the screen.

Line 40 initializes K, X, and Z. K is changed within the program from 2 to 1 and back again to form the basis of selecting the caterpillar string (L$(K)). X is a constant -1 as a device to cause Z to become alternately $+1$ and -1 when line 130 is executed within the program loops.

The main program loop 110 to 150 causes the caterpillar to move 17 places across the screen. The movement is caused in line 120 by progressively printing a longer and longer portion of the string s$ immediately in front of the caterpillar l$.

Within the main loop, there is the loop 112 to 145 which alternately prints the two caterpillar strings. Line 115 clears the screen and moves the cursor down five lines on each occasion to make sure that the pictures are superimposed correctly. Line 120 prints a version of the caterpillar preceded by the appropriate number of spaces according to the current value of i within the loop. Line 125 is a delay line to allow time for each caterpillar position to be viewed. Each time through the loops, at line 130, z is multiplied by −1. This causes z to become $1 \times -1 = -1, -1 \times -1 = 1, 1 \times -1 = -1, -1 \times -1 = 1$, etc. The value of κ in line 140 therefore becomes $2 - 1 = 1, 1 + 1 = 2, 2 - 1 = 1$, etc. on each execution of the loops. By this means, the appropriate l$ string, l$ (1) or l$ (2), is printed in line 120.

This has been explained in some detail as you can use the logic of lines 40, 130 and 140 in your own animations when you want some part of the picture to alternate.

If your computer has colour, try out different coloured caterpillars.

Patterns

This program makes use of the colour facilities of the vic to produce mosaic designs. If your computer does not have colour, you could still obtain patterned effects by using a variety of character symbols. The logic of the program and the basis of its patterns are best described on a small scale using letters of the alphabet for different colours.

The program produces a pattern by creating 'mirror images' of an initial sequence. Let us consider a mosaic of six characters by six. For the first line the computer would pick *three* characters at random, say, A, B and C. These three characters would then be reflected into the other three positions on the first line, that is:

ABCCBA

In the *second* line the first two characters move along one position and the original *second* character is also positioned first, that is:

BABBAB

The second half of the line is a 'reflection', as before.

In the *third* line the first two characters move one position, as before, and the original *third* character starts the line, that is:

CBAABC

The pattern so far is:

ABCCBA
BABBAB
CBAABC

The whole of this pattern is now reflected downwards to form the bottom three lines, giving:

ABCCBA
BABBAB
CBAABC
CBAABC
BABBAB
ABCCBA

The program for patterns is given in Table 5.4. The display is based on an eight by eight pattern giving a sixteen by sixteen mosaic when reflected. Line 10 dimensions the arrays (DIM). Line 20 clears the screen ready for the pattern to be displayed. In line 30, the variable A$ has a string of eight colour codes assigned to it. Line 40 moves the cursor down three lines from the home position to provide a border above the pattern. In lines 50 to 90, a random number (N) from 1 to 8 is generated; this is used as the basis for selecting one of the colour codes from string A$. This is repeated eight times so

Table 5.4 Patterns program

```
10 DIM O$(16,16)
20 PRINT"◻"
30 A$="◼◼◤◥◩◪◧◨"
40 PRINT"◼◼◼◼◼"
50 FOR I=1 TO 8
60 N=INT(RND(1)*8+1)
70 C$(I)=MID$(A$,N,1)
80 D$(I)=C$(I)
90 NEXT I
100 FOR L=1 TO 8
110 D$(1)=C$(L)
120 FOR P=8 TO 1 STEP -1
130 O$(P,L)=D$(P)
140 O$(17-P,L)=D$(P)
150 O$(P,17-L)=D$(P)
160 O$(17-P,17-L)=D$(P)
170 D$(P)=D$(P-1)
180 NEXT P
190 NEXT L
200 FOR L=1 TO 16
210 PRINT"   ";
220 FOR P=1 TO 16
230 PRINT O$(P,L)"◼ ";
240 NEXT P
250 PRINT
260 NEXT L
270 GOTO 40
```

that c$ ends up containing a random sequence of eight colour codes. The same sequence is also assigned to D$. During the program run C$ remains unchanged to provide a reference string, while D$ is manipulated as required for each successive line.

The pattern for the top half (eight lines) is developed within the loop 100 to 190. As the line number (L) is increased by the value one, so the first colour to be displayed (D$(1)) is set to C$(L). The loop, lines 120 to 180, then allocates the display codes in D$ to specific positions. Four assignment statements are used to place the contents of D$ into the four 'mirror image' positions. These positions are illustrated in terms of an initial position and line number in Figure 5.3. The value 17 occurs in the expression to allow the positions of columns 9–16 to be set up; as P varies from 8 to 1 the 'mirror' values will be $17 - 8 = 9$ to $17 - 1 = 16$.

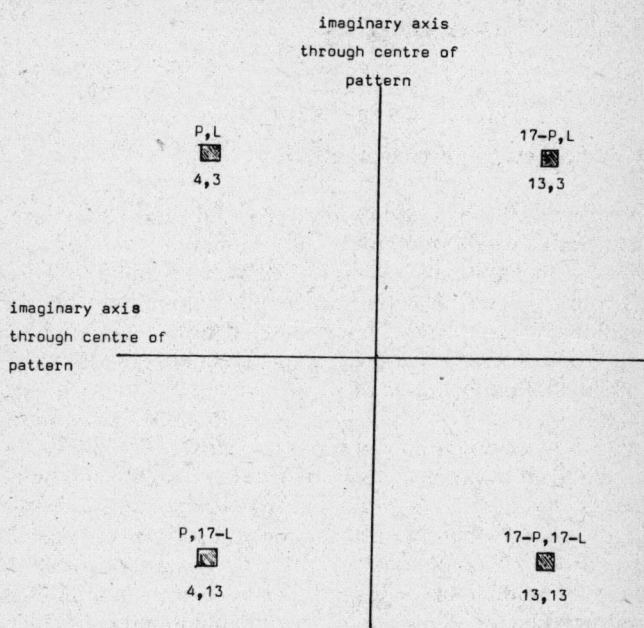

Figure 5.3 'Mirror images' of positions 4,3 in top left-hand quadrant

Line 170 advances the display codes along one position, leaving D$(1) containing a null (that is, empty) string. On looping back to 110, this first position has a colour code assigned to it, according to the line number, from C$.

The final part of the program, lines 200 to 260, prints out the array O$ within two loops. Line 230 prints a reverse space character in the colour of the code contained in O$(P,L). Line 270 causes the program to repeat from line 40, which has the effect of overlaying the existing pattern on the screen with a new, randomly generated pattern.

6   How Robots Work

Human and robot characteristics

The robots that you see in films or on television have been designed to look something like humans – they are humanoid in appearance and in their actions and reactions. However, in real life robots are mainly used in industry, for example, in car production. Industrial robots look nothing like humans and to a large extent do not behave like humans.

Humans are fortunate in having five senses – sight, touch, taste, smell and hearing – and a brain that has unique powers of observation, memory and analytical ability far surpassing any other living being's. We can design and build robots that can carry out a limited number of operations better than we can do them, but only in some areas. As our knowledge of technology advances, robots will be able to perform more complex tasks. Their range of capabilities is restricted by the 'senses' that we can build into them.

If you think carefully of how you do even the simplest task, you will understand how difficult it is to build a robot which could do the same task. Young children often have a toy consisting of a number of differently shaped holes in a 'work bench' with coloured pieces to be fitted into the correct holes. This 'learning' game was designed to teach children about shapes and colours and to improve their dexterity – how to fit things together properly. It is difficult to make a robot that can pick up an item, put it in the correct slot and do this in the most efficient way without too much trial and error.

First of all, it is difficult for a robot to select the correct item from a number of different items. Robots are fitted with sensors to respond to certain situations, for example, whether an item is present. Various types of sensor are available.

Physical contact with objects can be detected by pressure-sensitive devices. Others which respond to changes in a light beam are called photoelectric devices.

A photoelectric device can also be used to distinguish between a transparent or an opaque object. Another type of sensor, known as an inductive sensor, on the other hand, can detect changes in magnetic fields and therefore can be used to distinguish between objects made from brass or steel, when these are placed near it, because of their different magnetic properties. These signals can be fed back to a computer for processing. The computer can then send a signal to the robot to cause it to move its 'arm' and 'hand' to grip the piece and lift it to its correct position.

In an industrial situation, the object to be moved could be a heavy piece of metal, but this would not necessarily present a problem as sufficient electric or hydraulic power could be used to lift the arm easily.

The robot's ability to place an object the 'right way' around again is limited, and industrial robots generally have the workpiece to be machined presented to them in the correct position.

Just as humans can memorize a sequence of operations, so can we program a robot to follow a set of instructions. However, the human operator can also observe things going wrong, whereas the robot must be fitted with sensors to detect abnormal situations and be programmed to shut down the machine it is using or send a warning message to the factory supervisor.

It is possible now to have automated factories controlled by robots under the supervision of one or two human operators, whose job may involve starting/setting up machines and dealing with breakdowns. Using robots has a number of advantages. For example, whereas human operators need rest periods and can work for only limited shifts, robots can continue to work indefinitely, apart from non-productive periods (known as 'downtime') due to breakdowns or routine maintenance.

Human operators can work only in conditions that are not

too hot or too cold, with sufficient space to move comfortably and with enough air and light. There are minimum working conditions which employers must provide for their employees. Robots, on the other hand, can be designed to work in extreme conditions, for example, in a narrow space and in a poisonous atmosphere.

Industrial robots

The robots we see in films can move about freely. Although some robots in industry are designed to move about the factory floor in a limited way, most industrial robots remain fixed in position and have just a single moving arm. An example is shown in Figure 6.1.

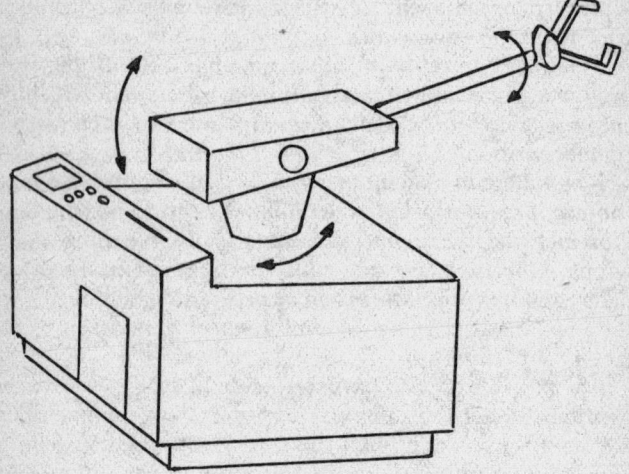

Figure 6.1   An industrial robot

The arm may move in three planes over a wide work area so that the robot can operate several machines in turn. Different 'hands' may be inserted at the 'wrist' end of the arm for gripping different objects or for scooping up powders and liquids.

Alternatively, the hand may be a tool for drilling, welding or spraying, or an electromagnet for picking up and dropping objects. Thin materials can be handled by using vacuum cups made of an elastic material. A vacuum seal can grip very tightly, as you know if you have tried to open a vacuum-sealed jar, without damaging the material. As the vacuum is released, the seal is broken and the 'hand' lets go of the material.

Robots are expensive to build, so flexibility is provided not only through interchangeable hands but also by having a selection of computer programs for controlling a variety of tasks automatically.

The arm, wrist and hand of the robot provide the strength and dexterity needed. These capabilities can be superior to the physical abilities of the human operator, since the robot can be engineered to lift heavy weights without tiring and position pieces very accurately under computer control. The programs stored in the computer's memory give the robot its intelligence, but remember these programs have been written by humans and are only as good as the logic devised and tested by the computer programmers. Computers and various memories are available now on single semi-conductor chips. This means that the computer controlling the robot's actions is small enough to be placed inside the robot.

Future robots

Robotics – the technology of designing robots and expanding their use into new areas – is a major new industry and developments are taking place which will give robots enhanced capabilities.

One of the main improvements required is giving robots a sense of vision. The robot needs to be given information as to where an object is (known as 'location data') and what it is (known as 'recognition data'). This may be done in the future by taking video pictures and analysing them precisely by a computer, which then instructs the robot to move as required.

Humans have two arms which can be used together in a co-ordinated way; also we can move around, speak and listen to each other. All these activities can be built into a robot, although speech recognition is still largely experimental. However, artificially produced speech (known as 'speech synthesis') has been developed for industrial use and it is possible for robots to be programmed to speak messages when they are activated by certain events, for example, if the machine they are feeding becomes jammed.

Applications

Robots are already being used for handling materials and loading machines, and for processes in manufacturing, such as casting, welding, moulding and spray painting.

In the future, we will see more 'unmanned' factories, where robots insert and remove parts from machines, assemble machined parts, automatically inspect parts and finished assemblies, and readjust equipment settings when faults are detected. This will become more possible when parts are designed with regard to the capabilities of the 'robot workers'.

We may also see robots being used in the home for some household tasks and as aids for the disabled. However, one of the main uses will be in industries where the work is unpleasant, repetitive or needs to take place in environments unsuitable for people.

Computer control

Controlling a robot by means of a computer program is not as difficult as it appears. At the back of most microcomputers you will see one or more connectors called input/output (i/o) ports to which equipment can be connected. One of these i/o ports may be used for a printer or disk drive unit. It is also possible – and fun – to connect models, such as a lift or a crane operated by an electric motor.

Programs can be written in machine code or BASIC which access the i/o port. The port will have a number of communication lines which can send signals to the model to control the motor (start, stop, reverse) or switch lights on and off. These lines will have been set to 'output'. Lines set to 'input' can receive signals from the model from sensors, and these signals can then be analysed by the computer and acted upon. For example, you may want to heat up some water using an electric heater. The temperature of the water can be measured by a sensor called a thermocouple, which is made from two dissimilar metals. A temperature change at the junction of the two metals causes a change in the voltage output from the thermocouple circuit. The output from the thermocouple can be linked to a computer to control the heating circuits.

The computer can accept only digital signals that are set to one of two conditions – high or low voltages (such as 5 volts or 0 volts) to represent a binary 1 or 0. Thermocouples give a continuous voltage output (this is known as an analog signal) and this needs to be converted to a digital signal before putting it onto the i/o port of the computer. This may be done using an analog to digitial (a/d) converter.

Quite simple programs can be used to illustrate how a computer can output a combination of signals to switch on lights or motors and to accept signals as input from switches or sensors. Your physics teacher will be able to help you if you want to construct a model or robot and control it with your computer.

In industry, however, robots are 'programmed' by people who are not necessarily familiar with computer programming. Special languages are available for use with industrial robots which make it easy for operators to program the robots for particular tasks. We will illustrate this in the next section, which gives a computer program to allow you to move a 'robot' around a 'factory floor', as represented on the screen of your computer.

Using the ROBOT program

When you run the program shown in Table 6.1, you will see initially the 'robot' near the bottom of the screen on the left side and four work benches. A solid square shown on one of the work benches will indicate the robot's destination.

You can cause the robot to move to its destination by giving it a sequence of up to 21 instructions as a string of characters. L or R moves the robot through 90° to the left or right, and T causes the robot to face the other way (it turns through 180°). F followed by a number between 1 and 9 moves the robot forward the given number of spaces. For example,

RF8F2LF2

would turn the robot to face right, then move it forward 10 spaces (across the screen), turn it to the left and move it forward 2 spaces (up the screen). Figure 6.2 shows a robot in the process of obeying a similar set of instructions. The upward arrows indicate the instructions that have been obeyed.

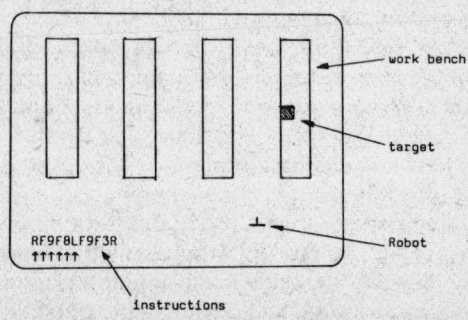

Figure 6.2   Robot and work bench

There are three possible outcomes:

1 All the instructions have been followed by the robot, but it has not reached its destination facing the right way; the message END OF INSTRUCTIONS will be displayed on the screen.
2 The robot 'crashes' into a work bench; the message YOU HAVE CRASHED will appear on the screen.
3 The robot reaches its destination facing the right way, that is, it finishes facing the solid square.

Outcomes (1) or (2) mean the robot has not completed its task, so it will be returned to its original position to allow you to instruct it again to reach the *same* destination.

If the robot reaches its destination, then the solid square will change so that it has a white ring on it, and the message JOB COMPLETE will appear on the screen. A new destination will be selected automatically at random and you will be able to direct the robot again.

Details of ROBOT Program (Table 6.1)

Line 10 changes the screen to light green and the border to black. Line 20 sets the values in the D array (for 'direction') to −22 (up), +1 (right), +22 (down) and −1 (left); these values are used in lines 1030 and 1055 to move the robot (R) in the required direction.

Line 30 sets the values in the C array (for 'correct orientation') to 113, 107, 114 and 115; these values are used to display the robot in the correct orientation (facing up, right, down or left) in lines 185, 1050 and 1560.

Lines 40 to 70 select the robot's destination (value of L), which is used in line 1570 to display a purple square on a work bench in the selected position.

Line 80 sets the initial screen position and orientation (facing up the screen) of the robot; this is used in line 1560 of the subroutine (lines 1500 to 1580) which also colours the robot blue.

Table 6.1 Robot program

```
10 POKE 36879,216
20 D(1)=-22:D(2)=1:D(3)=22:D(4)=-1
30 C(1)=113:C(2)=107:C(3)=114:C(4)=115
40 FOR I=1 TO 8:READ RN:RN(I)=7700+RN:NEXT I
50 DATA 5,6,10,11,15,16,20,21
60 L1=INT(8*RND(1)+1):L2=INT(12*RND(1))
70 L=RN(L1)+22*L2
80 R=8098:D=1
85 GOSUB 1500
90 INPUT "XXINSTRUCTIONS";R$
95 IF LEN(R$)<22 THEN 110
100 PRINT "XNOT MORE THAN 21"
105 FOR I=1 TO 1000:NEXT I:GOTO 85
110 GOSUB 1500
115 PRINT "SMMMMMMMMMMMMMMMMMMMMMMM";R$
120 A=1
125 POKE 8164,30:POKE 8164+38400-7680,4
130 A$=MID$(R$,A,1)
140 IF A$="F" THEN GOSUB 1000
150 IF A$="L" THEN D=D+3
160 IF A$="R" THEN D=D+1
170 IF A$="T" THEN D=D+2
175 IF D>4 THEN D=D-4
180 FOR J=1 TO 500:NEXT J
185 POKE R,C(D)
190 A=A+1:IF A>LEN(R$) THEN K=1:GOTO 2000
195 POKE 8163+A,30:POKE 8163+38400-7680+A,4
200 GOTO 130
1000 A=A+1
1005 POKE 8163+A,30:POKE 8163+38400-7680+A,4
1010 N=VAL(MID$(R$,A,1))
1020 FOR I=1 TO N
1030 R=R+D(D)
1035 IF PEEK(R)=32 THEN 1050
1040 IF PEEK(R)=96 THEN 1050
1045 K=2:GOTO 2000
1050 POKE R,C(D):POKE R+38400-7680,6
1055 POKE R-D(D),32
1060 FOR J=1 TO 500:NEXT J
1065 NEXT I
1070 RETURN
1500 PRINT "J"
1510 PRINT "   ⌐  ⌐  ⌐   ⌐ "
1520 FOR I=1 TO 10
1530 PRINT "   | |  | |  | |   | | "
1540 NEXT I
1550 PRINT "   ⌊  ⌊  ⌊   ⌊ "
1560 POKE R,C(D):POKE R+38400-7680,6
1570 POKE L,160:POKE L+38400-7680,4
1580 RETURN
```

```
2000 IF K=1 THEN Q$="END OF INSTRUCTIONS"
2010 IF K=2 THEN Q$="YOU HAVE CRASHED"
2020 PRINT "█████████████████";Q$
2025 IF K=1 THEN 2040
2030 FOR I=1 TO 12000:NEXT I:GOTO 80
2040 IF R-L=22 AND D=1 THEN 2500
2050 IF R-L=-1 AND D=2 THEN 2500
2060 IF R-L=-22 AND D=3 THEN 2500
2070 IF R-L=1 AND D=4 THEN 2500
2100 GOTO 2030
2500 POKE L,215:FOR I=1 TO 1000:NEXT I
2510 PRINT "JOB COMPLETE        "
2600 FOR I=1 TO 4000:NEXT I:RUN
```

Line 90 asks for instructions to be input. If more than 21 instructions are entered, a message is displayed (line 100) and, after a suitable time delay (line 105), you are given a chance to enter a new set of instructions.

The current position in the set of instructions is indicated by A (set to 1 initially in line 120). An upward purple arrow (↑) placed underneath an instruction (using lines 125, 195 or 1005) indicates that the instruction is being obeyed. The instructions are selected one at a time (line 130) and tested for F (line 140) or orientation (L, R or T in lines 150, 160 or 170). D is set to 1, 2, 3 or 4 in lines 150 to 175 to give the robot's orientation so that it is correctly displayed in line 185 after a time delay (line 180).

Subroutine 1000 to 1070 moves the robot forward by the given number of spaces N (line 1010), using lines 1020 to 1065. Lines 1035 and 1040 test if the robot (R) is on a space (ASCII character code 32 or 96). If it is not then the message YOU HAVE CRASHED is displayed (lines 2010 and 2020).

The position in the string of instructions is incremented by 1 and tested to see if the last of the instructions has been obeyed (line 190), in which case the message END OF INSTRUCTIONS is displayed (lines 2000 and 2020).

If the robot has crashed, it is repositioned to its start position after a long time delay (line 2030) to allow you to copy from the screen the instructions used.

When the end of the instructions has been reached, the

robot's position and orientation with respect to its destination (L) is tested. If the robot is facing the purple square, the latter is changed to display a white ring (line 2500) and the message JOB COMPLETE is displayed. After a time delay, the program is run again.

7 Making Computer Systems Secure

Computer security

Computers in industry and commerce can hold a large amount of information that is of great importance to the success of the companies' activities. Although the systems can be insured against hazards such as fire, flood, lightning, and so on, the loss of programs and data files is disastrous. Organizations therefore take special care as to where they locate their computer, make sure they have copies of their programs and data files stored in a different location, and also take steps to prevent unauthorized people gaining access to these files.

Smaller equipment, such as microcomputers, is easily portable and could be stolen unless it is kept in rooms which are protected by an alarm system. In a college or school, for instance, all pieces of equipment in the micro laboratory may be linked into an alarm system, which will sound whenever a person attempts to remove any part of that equipment. Warning notices in the room also act as a deterrent.

When you use a stand-alone (that is, a single-user) micro-computer with your own files of data and programs, you can take some security procedures yourself. For example, you learnt in Chapter 1 about preventing floppy disks being overwritten by covering or uncovering the notch in the disk, depending on the type of disk you are using. You should also make copies of your files in case a hardware or software fault occurs and accidentally damages or erases a magnetic tape or disk.

If the fault is due to hardware failure, then usually a trained engineer needs to repair and test the equipment. A software fault means the program causing it will need to be corrected. However, you should make another copy of the file that was erased so that you have two good copies again before testing the amended program.

If you don't want other people to look at, change or copy your programs and data, you can take away your tapes or disks and lock them up. Also, you need to make sure that you have cleared the information from the computer's memory either by switching the computer off or by typing a command, for example, NEW in BASIC.

On larger time-sharing systems, special procedures are used for making sure that all important files are copied (this is known as 'dumping') to tape or disk at frequent intervals. Computer service engineers inspect the computer equipment on a regular basis (once a week, fortnight or month) for routine maintenance. This is done to prevent faults developing, and results in a reliable service being provided for the many users of the system.

When many people have access to a computer system, it is necessary to make sure that users cannot 'read' one another's confidential files or obtain information from the computer to which they are not authorized. In practice, users are given their own unique codes which indicate to the computer how much of the system can be made available to them. A user code can also be used by the computer for other aspects of managing the system. For example, users may be charged for the amount of processor, peripheral and terminal time they use. This information may be logged on disk by the operating system against each user code and can then be processed by a program for accounting purposes.

A typical time-sharing computer, which has a complex operating system to control access to and use of the computer, is described in the next section. The examples given are for a particular system and details may vary.

The user's identification

The number issued to a user consists of three parts. The first part, consisting of from one to four digits, is used to represent an account number or a department, for example 007. The second part, consisting of from one to four alphanumeric characters (letters and numbers), can be used to indicate a sub-grouping, for example, MI5. These two parts are called the qualifier. The third part is a unique identifier for that user and can consist of from one to six alphanumeric characters, for example, BOND.

Whenever a user wishes to use a terminal, the computer puts the question USER NUMBER? on the terminal's screen. The user then types in his user code, for example:

007MI5 BOND

and the computer checks its files to make sure that this is a valid and allocated number.

Controlling users

Before a user can use a number, that number has to be set up in the system. When this is being done, eight further types of information are recorded against the user number in the computer files. These are:

1 The user's level of access represented by a number between one and fifteen (known as the 'access level'). The higher the access level allocated, the greater the range of files available.
2 A limit on the maximum size of the user's program area.
3 A time limit on any programs run by the user. This makes sure that programs that have gone into endless loops or otherwise 'run away', usually because of a logical error, will be stopped by the operating system.
4 A similar limit on the amount of the output from any program.
5 An execution priority level. This makes sure that certain

users' programs with higher priority levels are executed more quickly than those having a lower priority in a time-sharing system.

6 A central processing time limit. This keeps the time spent by a user below an allocated maximum.

7 The amount of space allowed for storing information (that is, programs and data) on the disk units.

8 Access code. This code indicates which particular peripheral devices, such as special printers and graph plotters, may be used.

These controls have two purposes. Firstly, to prevent users from having uncontrolled access to the computer system; this could result in inexperienced users accidentally erasing programs or data or allow other users to gain access to confidential information. Secondly, to make sure the system runs smoothly by allocating various aspects of the computer's resources to users according to their needs.

User control

Users can exercise control over 'their' parts of the system. Passwords can be created or changed at any time by the user to make sure that other users, even though they may know the user's number, cannot access his files. A password is created by simply entering CPASS followed by the password:

CPASS,XRAY

To change this password, the old password is preceded by the new one:

CPASS,LASER,XRAY

When a user creates some data, it can only be read, altered or deleted by that user unless certain conditions have been attached to the data. For example, the set of data (called a file) can, if required, be made available to all users to read, write or delete; this is known as Public Read, Public Write,

Public Delete. Normally, a user would allow others to read the data but not write to it or delete it. In addition, the user can set the access level for any file created.

To create a file called BOOKS and have an access level of 5, the user would enter the following at the terminal:

GENERATE BOOKS,ACCESS=5

A user cannot specify an access level higher than his own. At a later stage, when the file has suitable information written to it, the user may wish to make the file available to others (the 'public'). This step is achieved by respecifying the file (Re-Type) as Public Read by entering:

RT BOOKS PR

User-friendly software

Another aspect of computer security is to make sure that the programs run correctly. It is difficult and tedious to make programs completely foolproof, but it is important to help the person who is going to use the program to run it successfully. You can make a program user-friendly by making it easy to use and providing menus, as described in Chapter 3, and by identifying incorrect entries made by the user.

Input statements should be written to initiate the correct response and to trap unacceptable responses where possible. For example, you can indicate that a date should be entered (into D$) with two digits for the day, month and year separated by oblique signs by using the following input statement:

100 INPUT "DATE (DD/MM/YY)";D$

By putting an input statement within a loop, you can make sure that only *acceptable* responses are accepted. For example, if the expected input is a Y (for yes) or an N (for no) any other response will cause the input to be requested again if the following loop is used:

```
100 PRINT "ENTER Y OR N"
110 INPUT A$
120 IF A$ = "Y" THEN 200
130 IF A$ = "N" THEN 300
140 GOTO 100
```

In the above example, line 140 traps any unacceptable response.

A further aspect to consider is that an expected abbreviation, for example Y, may instead be spelt out in full, in this case as YES. The coding shown above will not accept YES for Y. While this does not cause the program to go wrong, a user who responds with a YES can get annoyed and the program does not appear user-friendly. A slight change in the coding allows Y or YES to be equally acceptable – similarly N or NO; this is achieved by testing for the initial letter of the response. The changes required are:

```
120 IF LEFT$(A$,1) = "Y" THEN 200
130 IF LEFT$(A$,1) = "N" THEN 300
```

This will of course allow *any* word beginning with Y or N to be accepted as a correct response. You can restrict the responses to Y or YES and N or NO by using the logical operation OR, as shown in the following revised versions of lines 120 and 130:

```
120 IF A$ = "Y" OR A$ = "YES" THEN 200
130 IF A$ = "N" OR A$ = "NO" THEN 300
```

You may be tempted to use a GET statement for accepting the single character Y or N as follows:

```
100 PRINT "ENTER Y OR N"
110 GET A$ : IF A$ = "" THEN 110
120 IF A$ = "Y" THEN 200
130 IF A$ = "N" THEN 300
140 GOTO 100
```

In this case, line 110 contains a loop that keeps the computer executing line 110 until A$ becomes something other than a null string. As soon as Y of an intended YES response is keyed

in, the routine is left via line 120 to line 200. Although this
method works well in principle, it can confuse users who
may not be looking at the screen while they are slowly typing
in Y E S. When they look up the program has already executed
line 200 and beyond! This method would therefore not be
user-friendly for unskilled operators, although GET is useful
where a single key response is required, as in some of the
examples in Chapter 4.

Secret messages

The need to pass secret messages dates back to the earliest
times, particularly during wars. If a message were in a secret
code, its contents could not be deciphered even if the messen-
ger were captured.

Today, many companies and nations have important
information on computers, and often some of this information has to be sent via communications systems, such as by
telephone lines and satellites, to other computers. If the
communication links were tapped, unauthorized people
could possibly obtain information that could be used to harm
or blackmail the senders. So even today there is still sometimes a need to send computer information in a secret, coded
form.

As computers are very fast, the methods used to code and
decode messages can be very complex compared to the
simple methods people use. However, the earlier methods,
like the one in the following section, can still be quite effective
if you want to use them on your personal computer.

Caesar's cipher

Julius Caesar used a code that replaced every letter in the
message by the letter three places ahead of it in the alphabet;
B became E, and so on, and letters at the end of the alphabet

were followed by the beginning of the alphabet so that X, Y and Z became A, B and C.

Although Caesar shifted the letters forwards by three, you can choose to shift them by any number you like, forwards *or* backwards. The program shown in Table 7.1 asks you to enter the amount of shift required in line 20. This could be, for example, 3 or −3.

Table 7.1 Coding and decoding program

```
10 REM CAESAR'S CIPHER
20 PRINT "INPUT SHIFT";:INPUT K:PRINT
30 PRINT "CODE OR DECODE";
40 INPUT R$
50 IF LEFT$(R$,1)="C" THEN S=+K
60 IF LEFT$(R$,1)="D" THEN S=-K
65 IF LEFT$(R$,1)<CHR$(67) THEN 30
68 IF LEFT$(R$,1)>CHR$(68) THEN 30
70 PRINT:PRINT "ENTER MESSAGE"
80 PRINT
90 INPUT M$
100 L=LEN(M$)
110 FOR I=1 TO L
120 A$=MID$(M$,I,1)
130 X=ASC(A$)
132 IF X=32 THEN 160
135 X=X+S
140 IF X>=91 THEN X=X-58
150 IF X<=32 THEN X=X+58
160 C$=C$+CHR$(X)
170 NEXT I
180 PRINT
190 PRINT
200 PRINT "RESULT :-"
210 PRINT
220 PRINT C$
230 END
```

The program allows you to either code or decode a message and you respond to the PRINT statement in line 30 by entering C or D. If you are coding, the shift you entered, the variable K in line 20, is copied to variable s unchanged (line 50). If you are decoding, the direction of shift is changed by setting s to −K (line 60).

If the ASCII character code for "C" or "D" (CHR$ 67 and

CHR$ 68) has not been input then the program repeats the input request from line 30.

The message to be coded or decoded is entered into M$ at line 90 in response to line 70. Line 100 establishes the length of the message (L) so that the coding/decoding routine for an individual character (lines 120 to 160) is repeated L times. Within the loop (lines 110 to 170) each character is extracted in turn from the message by use of a MID$ statement (line 120) and stored in A$. X is set to the ASCII character code (line 130) equivalent to the character held in A$. If the character was a space (ASCII character code 32) then X will equal 32, and no change to the space is required. In these cases, line 132 directs the computer to line 160, where the revised message is being built up, and adds on the unchanged space character.

In this program, only the space character is left unchanged. Other characters, such as full stops, colons, etc., are treated like letters of the alphabet and are automatically 'shifted' to become another character. This applies to all characters whose ASCII codes lie between 33 (!) and 90 (z). For example, character ! (ASCII code 33) shifted forwards four places becomes character % (ASCII code 37).

Line 135 shifts the character code (X) by the required amount (S). If this revision of X takes it outside the range 33 to 90 then a wrap-around effect is achieved by adding 58 (i.e. 33 to 90 *inclusive*) or subtracting 58 as required (lines 140 and 150). For example, if the letter Y (character code 89) is to be shifted two character codes forward, the revised character code is 91 (i.e. 89 + 2). As this is greater than 90, 58 is subtracted, giving a character code of 33 which represents the exclamation symbol (!).

After building up the required message, C$, in line 160 within the loop, the contents of C$ finally is printed in line 220.

Ideas for development

Enter the program in Table 7.1 into your computer and
check that it works as intended. For example, check that you
get similar results to those shown in Table 7.2 and Table 7.3.

Table 7.2   Coding a message

```
INPUT SHIFT? 2
CODE OR DECODE? C
ENTER MESSAGE
? MEET BY THE GYM AT 5.00
RESULT :-
OGGV D! VJG I!D CV 7022
```

Table 7.3   Decoding a message

```
INPUT SHIFT? 2
CODE OR DECODE? D
ENTER MESSAGE
? OGGV D! VJG I!0 CV 7022
RESULT :-
MEET BY THE GYM AT 5.00
```

A simple way of using this program is to write down the
output and pass it as a coded message to your friends. They
then will decode it on their own computer.

Better still is to pass the message on cassette tape, so it
cannot be read. To do this you need two versions of the
program. The coding version takes the message in, as before,
from the keyboard (line 90) but outputs the coded message
(in line 220) to tape. You need to add two lines, say line 85 to
OPEN a cassette tape file in WRITE mode on your system and
line 225 to CLOSE the file. Line 220 needs to be changed to
print to a file. Table 7.4 shows the required changes for a
coding system.

Table 7.4 Amendments for cassette version of coding program

```
85 OPEN 1,1,1
220 PRINT#1,C$
225 CLOSE 1
```

The other version of the program, to decode a message on tape, requires the file to be OPENed for READing and CLOSEd as before, but line 90 now inputs from tape and line 220 remains unchanged, outputting to the screen. Table 7.5 shows the required changes for a decoding program.

Table 7.5 Amendments for cassette version of decoding program

```
85 OPEN 1,1,0
90 INPUT#1,M$
225 CLOSE 1
```

To make it harder for an enemy to decode, the number of characters shifted should be changed in an agreed way. For example, you can agree in advance with your friends that the shift value will be two days ahead of the current day of the month.

When you've tried out this program, you could try programming some of the other codes given in code books.

8 Keeping Records

Records, files and data bases

The main use of computers all over the world is for processing business information. This type of application is called commercial data processing.

Generally, the data to be processed consists of records containing a number of related items, or fields. For example, if you were a club secretary/treasurer, you may want to keep a file of records. The file could be a box of cards, each card holding information about one club member, or you could create a file on cassette or disk using your computer. Each record could contain the name, address and telephone number of the club members, with some extra information that you could use for particular purposes. You may want to include club members' interests so that you could pick out people who could help you to put on certain events. Another useful piece of information could be a note of whether they have paid their subscriptions, and you could use this to send reminders to members whose subscriptions are due and also to keep your accounts.

Companies may keep many different files of business information. This is stored usually on disk, although magnetic tape may be used for storing information that is not currently in use but may need to be referred to occasionally. Some companies set up data bases on disk for holding all items of information which may be used by different programs. Although each program may use only some of the information, using a data base avoids having a variety of files with duplicated information. This allows several different application programs to use a common set of data. For

example, employee data may be used by programs processing personnel records *and* payroll records.

One advantage of holding all a company's information on
a data base is that when any changes are made to items, all
the different application programs using the data base will
have the same up-to-date information. Keeping separate files
with duplicated information can mean that not all files are
revised, that is, updated, at the same time and are out of step.

Another advantage of having a company data base is that
the information held on it can be controlled more easily than
if separate files were used. One person, the data base admin-
istrator (DBA), or a team of people, can be put in charge of the
company's data. They can make sure that the information on
the data base is kept up to date and secure. They
will need to set up security procedures, as mentioned in
Chapter 7.

Company data bases can be very large and take up a large
amount of disk storage. The DBA has to have technical
knowledge on how the data base is constructed and used, so
that the data can be stored and processed in the best way.
The DBA has to organize the data base so that the storage is
kept to a minimum and the fastest possible processing speeds
are obtained for the different applications.

A large company data base will be set up and controlled by
means of a complex set of programs called a data base
management system (DBMS). Simpler data base software may
be available on your school computer if it has a disk unit.

Your home computer may be equipped with only one
cassette recorder, and this makes it difficult to use for file
processing. However, you can try the programs described
later in this chapter on your computer as examples of some of
the processes that are carried out in commercial data processing.

Commercial data processing

Systems analysis and design

With any computer application, the first thing that needs to be done is to carry out an investigation of the problem. We need to consider what results are required from the computer system, the data that is needed to achieve these results, how the data should be entered, by whom, and in what form output will be needed. Finally, we must determine the processing that needs to be done to achieve the required results from the available data. This investigation is called systems analysis. For a large commercial system, this investigation can take a team of systems analysts several months or more than a year to complete.

The systems analysis stage is very important and must be carried out to arrive at an efficient systems design, which is later converted into computer programs. These computer programs will become an operational system to be used for processing data at regular intervals. The programs must be designed to process the data efficiently and correctly. Another essential part of the system development, therefore, is program design and testing. The systems analyst will select typical data for testing each program in the system. When each program has been proved to be working correctly, the programs must be shown to produce the correct results when working together as a system.

If a system is difficult to use, mistakes can be made by the people using it. As you learnt in Chapter 3, a good man/ machine interface is very important. Modern techniques of systems analysis and design involve the eventual users of the system at an early stage. Users can try out proposed screen layouts and help the systems people to design a system that will be acceptable as well as efficient. Such a system is more likely to be successful.

Data entry and verification

Another feature of commercial data processing is the large amounts of data that need to be processed. This is one of the main differences that computer science students find when they start working in industry. The programs that you develop at school and later at college may be written in similar programming languages to those used in industry, but they will use relatively small amounts of data.

When large amounts of data are to be processed, it is important that the entry of data is speeded up, checked for accuracy, and made easy for the operator. We can illustrate some of the concepts by considering a simple program to enter names and addresses, etc. You may like to use this idea to set up your own files.

If we consider first the man/machine interface, we need to design a data entry screen layout that is easy to use on the

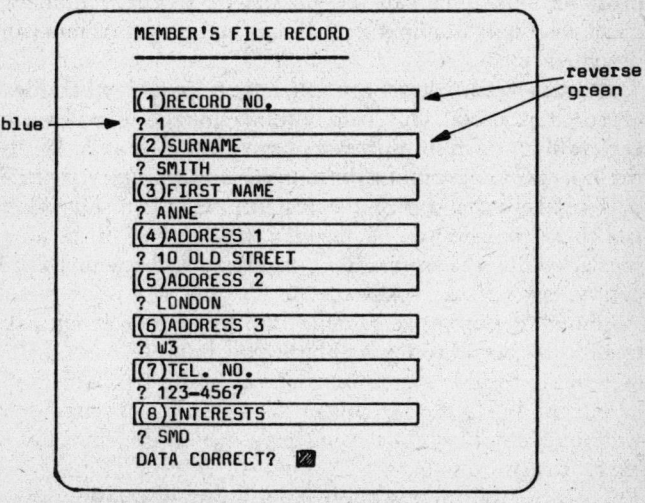

Figure 8.1   Data entry screen layout

equipment available. Most commercial data entry equipment has 80-column or larger screens. We are using the VIC-20 personal computer which has a 22-column screen. Although we are limited as to the amount of information that can be displayed on one line, we can make use of some of the special features of the VIC-20 to design an easy-to-use screen layout.

A good screen layout for a program that displays records of members of a club is shown in Figure 8.1. Colour is used to distinguish between prompts and the data entered by the user. The program itself is given in Table 8.1 and described from page 106.

In industry, data needs to be checked for accuracy. Data entry software may be used to prevent the operator from recording some wrong data. For example, numeric data may be accepted only if it falls within a certain range by setting what is known as a range check, such as 1 to 30 for a date in September. Some of the data fields may always contain numbers or always alphabetic characters or various known combinations. This can be checked by setting a contents check for each data field so that only certain characters will be accepted.

When a record has been entered, it should be verified before it is used. This can be done by the operator (or preferably a different operator) keying the data in again. If the two entries agree then the data is likely to be correct since it is unlikely that the same mistakes will be made twice. Another, less safe way of checking the accuracy of the data entered is for the operator to do a visual check and then correct any mistakes spotted.

Our data entry program allows the operator to change any line of data before recording the record on tape.

Updating files

There are basically two types of business information – permanent, or static, and changing. Static information would be the names and addresses of employees or customers, or descriptions and unit costs of items in stock. This information will change only occasionally. However, employees get paid weekly or monthly and their salary records, which show the total amount they have earned and tax and national insurance paid to date, need to be updated whenever their payslips are processed.

Similarly, customer records will need to be updated according to the orders they have placed and the amounts they have paid, so that invoices, receipts and statements (showing the amounts owing) can be sent to them.

Different programs that make up an application package or suite of application programs will be available for each system (payroll, order processing, etc.). There may be one data entry program which allows different 'forms' to be displayed on the screen. Each form may be set up to include various checks and verification on the different fields, as described previously. Usually, other programs will be used for the updating runs.

It is difficult to update a file when you have only one cassette recorder attached to your computer. You need to read your records into the computer's memory and store them there, make the required changes, and then output all the records as a new file to cassette.

If you have a disk unit, you can write programs to update files in a similar way to that used in industry. Just an outline of the procedure is given here.

The records on a disk file may be organized in such a way to enable programs to access them directly. On magnetic tape, records are accessed one after another in the same order in which they are recorded on the tape; this is known as serial access. A direct access file on disk has an index at the beginning of the file which 'points' to each record in the file. This means the update program can be written to access the record to be changed, transfer it to the computer's memory, change it in the memory and then write it back to the disk.

The same area of the disk may be used for the new record so that the old record is overwritten. The information on the old record therefore is lost unless a copy is made. Keeping copies of files for security purposes was mentioned in Chapter 7. Data security is an extremely important aspect of commercial data processing. Imagine how long it would take you to write out the club membership records for, say, 50 people; a company may have many thousands of customers and employees, for instance, so it's vital that no computer records are accidentally destroyed. In fact, even for the small amount of data processing that you may want to do, it's good practice to set up a system of keeping copies of programs and data files.

Reports

A third type of program, report programs, is used to produce output. An 'enquiry program' puts information on the screen related to particular records as selected by an enquirer. Alternatively, a 'report' program is written to produce printed lists, payslips, invoices, etc. Reports may be listed on the screen but are more often produced in printed form using one of the printers mentioned in Chapter 1 (page 12).

The program shown in Table 8.2 gives you some idea of how a file can be processed to produce a short list on the screen. This program is described on page 110. If you have access to a printer, you could change the program to produce a printed list.

Data processing programs

Data entry program

This program, shown in Table 8.1, has been designed to display a form on the screen so that names, addresses, telephone numbers and interests can easily be entered from the keyboard. At the end of each form you are asked whether the data is correct. If it is not, you are given the opportunity

Table 8.1 Data entry program

```
5 POKE 36879,216:PRINT "■"
10 PRINT "▮MEMBERS FILE"
20 PRINT "------------"
25 PRINT
30 PRINT "DATE (DD/MM/YY)"
35 INPUT DS$
40 PRINT
45 PRINT "▮PUT BLANK TAPE      IN RECORDER"
50 PRINT
55 PRINT "PRESS ANY KEY        TO CONTINUE"
60 PRINT
65 GET A$:IF A$="" THEN 65
70 OPEN 1,1,1,"MEMBERS"
80 PRINT#1,DS$
100 PRINT "▮MEMBER'S FILE RECORD"
110 PRINT "--------------------"
115 PRINT
120 PRINT "▮▮(1)RECORD NO.        "
130 PRINT "▮▮(2)SURNAME           "
140 PRINT "▮▮(3)FIRST NAME        "
150 PRINT "▮▮(4)ADDRESS 1         "
160 PRINT "▮▮(5)ADDRESS 2         "
170 PRINT "▮▮(6)ADDRESS 3         "
180 PRINT "▮▮(7)TEL. NO.          "
190 PRINT "▮▮(8)INTERESTS         "
200 PRINT "■"
300 FOR L=1 TO 8
310 ON L GOSUB 500,510,520,530,540,550,560,570
320 NEXT L
400 PRINT "▮▮▮▮▮▮▮▮▮▮▮▮▮▮▮▮▮▮▮▮▮▮"
410 INPUT "DATA CORRECT";Y$
420 IF Y$="Y" OR Y$="YES" THEN 600
430 PRINT "FIELD TO BE CORRECTED"
435 INPUT L
440 ON L GOSUB 500,510,520,530,540,550,560,570
450 GOTO 400
500 INPUT "▮▮▮▮▮▮";RN$
507 RETURN
510 INPUT "▮▮▮▮▮▮▮▮";S$:RETURN
520 INPUT "▮▮▮▮▮▮▮▮▮▮";F$:RETURN
530 INPUT "▮▮▮▮▮▮▮▮▮▮▮▮";A1$:RETURN
540 INPUT "▮▮▮▮▮▮▮▮▮▮▮▮▮▮";A2$:RETURN
550 INPUT "▮▮▮▮▮▮▮▮▮▮▮▮▮▮▮▮";A3$:RETURN
560 INPUT "▮▮▮▮▮▮▮▮▮▮▮▮▮▮▮▮";TN$:RETURN
570 INPUT "▮▮▮▮▮▮▮▮▮▮▮▮▮▮▮▮▮▮";IN$
580 RETURN
600 PRINT#1,RN$;",";S$;",";F$;",";A1$;",";A2$;
610 PRINT#1,",";A3$;",";TN$;",";IN$
615 IF RN$="0" THEN 700
620 GOTO 100
700 CLOSE 1
710 PRINT "▮PRESS STOP ON TAPE    AND REWIND"
```

of changing any line using the cursor controls. When the data is correct, the record is written to, that is, recorded on, the cassette tape.

You may create tapes on different days so each tape is identified by a date, entered at line 35 and written as the first record to the tape at line 80. The file is 'opened' for writing (this is indicated by the *third* 1 after the word OPEN) and then named in line 70. The name MEMBERS will be contained in the header of the file. Note that line 65 waits for an entry from the keyboard (requested at line 55) to allow you time to put a blank tape in the recorder.

Lines 120 to 190 put a form on the screen with the data field names shown against a green background (that is, in green reverse video) so that they are distinct from the data, as indicated in Figure 8.1. Line 200 sets 'writing' on the screen to blue with a colour control code.

Lines 300 to 320 move the cursor to the appropriate positions on the form for entry of data in each of the eight fields. Line 310 causes a branch to one of eight subroutines depending on the value of L. For example, if L = 1, line 500 is executed next. This positions the cursor at the beginning of the record number data field by moving it first to the home position and then down the required number of lines on the screen. A question mark (?) will appear underneath the data field name indicating that you should enter the record number (as shown in Figure 8.1). After you have entered the record number, line 507 will return to line 320 for the next value of L (2, or whatever, up to 8). When L = 2, line 510 (a complete subroutine on one line, as are all lines between 520 and 560) will allow you to enter a surname, and so on for the other six values of L. After eight items of data have been entered (and stored in variables RN$, S$, F$, A1$, A2$, A3$, TN$, IN$), the message:

DATA CORRECT?

will be displayed (line 410).

If you have made a mistake when entering the data, you

can correct this by replying N or NO (or in fact any response other than Y or YES). The message:

FIELD TO BE CORRECTED
?

will then be displayed (lines 430 and 435). You can then change any field by entering the number of the field to be changed (1 to 8) in response to the question mark (?). The cursor will now be positioned at the beginning of the data field to be corrected so that you can enter it again. The message DATA CORRECT? will appear as before to allow you to change another field or to indicate that all the fields are correct (by entering Y or YES).

When the data is correct, a branch is made to line 600 where the member's record is written to tape. The procedure is repeated for each member by the program returning to line 100 (at line 620). You should enter "0" for the last 'dummy' record number (to indicate end-of-file) and just press the return key for the other data fields to complete entry of this end-of-file record. The program tests for end-of-file, i.e. for RN$ = "0", at line 615. When RN$ contains 0, a branch is made to line 700 where the file is closed and you are asked to:

PRESS STOP ON TAPE
AND REWIND

Notes on data entry

Remember that in an INPUT statement you separate *different* data fields by commas. Therefore, using this program, you must *not* include any commas in your data fields as these will be interpreted as end-of-field.

Interest codes are S, M or D for sports, music or drama. A club member can have up to three interests recorded; these are put in as a string with no spaces between the codes, for example, SMD, SD, M.

You should now have a data tape for use with the report program described in the next section. Make sure that you label the tape with its name, MEMBERS, and the date.

Report program

This program, shown in Table 8.2, has been designed to produce a list of names and telephone numbers of club members who are interested in sports, music or drama. As club secretary, you could contact some of the members to help you organize a particular event.

The date of the required MEMBERS file (DF$) is entered at line 20. You will then be asked to put a cassette containing this file in the tape recorder (lines 25 to 40) and to press any key to continue (line 50). Line 60 waits for any entry from the keyboard in the same way as line 65 does in the data entry program shown in Table 8.1. The file is opened for *reading* at line 70; this is indicated by the third number after the word OPEN, which is now 0 instead of 1 (used in Table 8.1, line 70, for opening a file for *writing*).

Line 90 compares the data entered at line 20 with the date recorded at the beginning of the file. If the dates do not agree, the message WRONG FILE is displayed and the program is started again automatically after a time interval (lines 100 and 105). If the correct file has been loaded, the required interest code, s, M or D, in this case s, is entered in response to a message (lines 110 and 120) and stored in C$.

Lines 130 to 160 display headings at the top of the screen:

MEMBERS LIST (S)

NAME   TEL.NO.

Note that the second PRINT in line 140 causes a blank line to be left in the display under the first heading. The code shown in brackets after MEMBERS LIST, s, M or D, is displayed in purple with the rest of the printing in blue.

Each record on the file is read from the tape into the computer's memory (line 200) and tested for the required code (lines 210 to 230). Line 220 compares the member's interest codes (stored in IN$) with the required interest code contained in C$. Line 220 is within a loop (lines 210 to 230) which causes it to be executed one to three times depending

Table 8.2 Report program

```
10 POKE 36879,216:PRINT "■"
15 PRINT "⊃■DATE OF FILE(DD/MM/YY)"
20 INPUT DF$
25 PRINT "⊃PUT MEMBERS FILE"
30 PRINT TAB(5);"(";DF$;")"
40 PRINT "IN TAPE RECORDER"
45 PRINT
50 PRINT "PRESS ANY KEY        TO CONTINUE"
60 GET A$:IF A$="" THEN 60
70 OPEN 1,1,0,"MEMBERS"
80 INPUT#1,D$
90 IF D$=DF$ THEN 110
100 PRINT:PRINT "WRONG FILE"
105 FOR I=1 TO 3000:NEXT I:RUN
110 PRINT "⊃ENTER INTEREST CODE"
120 INPUT C$
130 PRINT "⊃MEMBERS LIST (■";C$;"■)"
140 PRINT "-----------------":PRINT
150 PRINT "NAME          TEL.NO."
160 PRINT "----          -------"
170 PRINT
200 INPUT#1,RN$,S$,F$,A1$,A2$,A3$,TN$,IN$
205 IF RN$="0" THEN 300
210 FOR I=1 TO LEN(IN$)
220 IF MID$(IN$,I,1)=C$ THEN 250
230 NEXT I
240 GOTO 200
250 PRINT F$;" ";S$;TAB(14);TN$
260 GOTO 200
300 CLOSE 1
310 PRINT "PRESS STOP ON TAPE    AND REWIND"
```

on the length of the IN$ string (line 210). The first time line 220 is executed, I will have the value 1 so that the *first* character in IN$ is compared with C$. If a match is found, the program branches to line 250. Otherwise, when IN$ contains more than one character, line 220 is repeated.

For example, if the contents of IN$ is SD and C$ contains D, then the first time line 220 is executed (with I = 1), S (the first character in IN$) would be compared with the D contained in C$ and no match would be found. The length of IN$ would be two, in this case, therefore line 220 would be repeated (with I = 2). This time the *second* character in IN$ (D) would be compared with the D in C$ and a match would be found.

When a match is found, the member's first name, surname and telephone number are listed on the screen under the headings NAME and TEL.NO. If no match is found for this member, then the program branches back to line 200 to read the next record on the cassette tape.

When the end-of-file is reached (that is, RN$="0"), as tested at line 205, the file is closed and you are asked to stop the tape and rewind it.

If you have a printer, you could amend the program to print the details and write another program to print names and addresses for sticking on to envelopes.

Appendix A

Glossary of BASIC

This appendix covers the BASIC language used in this book. It is *not* intended to replace the user manual supplied with your microcomputer. Most of the examples used in this appendix have been taken from the programs contained in the book. You should refer to these actual programs to appreciate how the individual BASIC statements are used in programs. A section on special features appears on page 130.

ASC
This function converts a string character to an ASCII code number.
For example:

    10 x = ASC("E")

results in x = 69, since the ASCII code number for "E" is 69.
The string character can be a string variable, as in:

    130 x = ASC(A$)

This line is used in the coding and decoding program (Table 7.1) to convert a string character in a secret message to a number.

CHR$
This function converts an ASCII code number into a string character.
For example:

    10 X$ = CHR$(69)

results in x$ = "E", since the ASCII code number for "E" is 69.

A further example of the use of CHR$ can be found in the noughts and crosses program (Table 4.2):

    3084 PRINT "PLAYER "; CHR$ (s+64); " HAS WON!"

In this program the two players (o and x) are represented by the variable s being either 15 or 24. PRINT CHR$(s+64) will therefore display either an o or an x character, since the ASCII code number for the letter o is 79 (i.e. 15 + 64) and for the letter x is 88 (i.e. 24 + 64).

CLOSE

A CLOSE statement is used together with an OPEN statement when processing files. Each file that is opened needs to be closed, after it has been finally processed, by a CLOSE statement, as in:

    700 CLOSE 1

The number following the CLOSE is the file number and should be the same as the number used in the corresponding OPEN statement.

DATA

DATA lines are used in conjunction with READ statements. Individual entries in DATA lines are separated by commas:

    20 DATA 10,27,1.5

(See READ for use of DATA statements in a program.)

DIM

The DIM statement is used to DIMension the main storage area to be used for arrays, as in:

    10 DIM A(20),B$(30)

This line ensures that sufficient storage is allocated in main memory to allow array A to contain up to twenty-one values (i.e. A(0), A(1), A(2), . . . A(20)). Similarly, B$ can contain up to thirty-one string variable values. In practice, the zero storage locations, i.e. A(0), B$(0), are seldom used.

The fizzy drinks program (Table 2.4) uses DIM to allow up to twelve names (N$), sizes (S) and prices (P) to be processed:

10 DIM N$(12),S(12),P(12)

An array needs to be dimensioned *before* it can be used, and therefore DIM statements should be positioned near the beginning of the program. An array can be dimensioned by a variable entered when the program is run. This is referred to as *dynamic dimensioning*. An example of this is found in Table 4.8:

40 INPUT "NO OF PLAYERS";N
60 DIM P$(N),S(N)

With the Commodore VIC you don't need to use a DIM statement for arrays whose dimensions are ten or less.

END
The END statement causes the computer to stop execution of the program, as in:

700 END

The END statement can be incorporated in an IF . . . THEN . . . instruction, as in Table 4.1:

165 IF A$ = "N" THEN END

There may be more than one END in a program, as the following lines from Table 4.9 illustrate:

170 IF N=1 THEN 190
180 PRINT "███";TAB(5);"WHITE WINS!":END
190 PRINT "███";TAB(5);"BLACK WINS!":END

FOR . . . NEXT
The FOR statement works with the NEXT statement so that the instructions between the FOR and the NEXT statements form a loop and are repeated a number of times. The full FOR statement has the form:

    FOR variable = expression 1 TO expression 2 STEP EXPRESSION 3

where expression 1 sets the initial value of the variable (which is the loop counter), expression 2 sets the final value of the loop counter and expression 3 gives the increment to be added to the variable at the end of each pass through the set of instructions in the loop. If STEP is equal to 1, both the word STEP and expression 3 may be omitted, e.g.

    15 FOR I=1 TO 26
    20 READ X$(I):NEXT I

(see Table 4.1).

    FOR . . . NEXT loops can be set up inside one another (this is called 'nesting'). The following example of nested loops, where the inner one also uses STEP to count down from 8 to 1, is taken from Table 5.4:

    100 FOR L=1 TO 8
    . . .
    120 FOR P=8 TO 1 STEP −1
    . . .
    . . .
    . . .
    180 NEXT P
    190 NEXT L

GET
The GET statement is used to obtain a *single* character from the keyboard. When GET is used in a program, the computer does not wait for the RETURN key to be pressed, as in:

    155 GET A$

The GET statement can be used to form a delay loop that causes the program to 'wait' at a line until a key is depressed. This method has been used in Table 4.2:

    5010 GET A$:IF A$="" THEN 5010

The program loops continuously at line 5010 until a

keyboard entry is made and A$ no longer is a null string (that is, contains nothing).

GOSUB

This statement is similar to a GOTO statement except that as the program is directed to a subroutine it will return from the subroutine to the line immediately following the GOSUB. This is useful if the program requires a routine to be used several times in different parts of the program, as in Table 3.1:

```
510 GOSUB 100
1020 GOSUB 100
1110 GOSUB 100
1210 GOSUB 100
etc.
```

The end of a subroutine is indicated by a RETURN statement:

```
150 RETURN
```

for the subroutine starting at line 100 in Table 3.1.

GOTO

The GOTO statement directs the program to the line number following the GOTO. For example:

```
10 PRINT "INPUT A NUMBER BETWEEN 1 AND 4"
20 INPUT N
30 IF N< 1 THEN 50
40 IF N =< 4 THEN 70
50 PRINT "OUTSIDE LIMITS"
60 GOTO 10
70 REM START CALCULATION
80 . . .
```

The above program will only start the calculation part when a number between 1 and 4 has been entered, otherwise the GOTO in line 60 causes the program to repeat the request for input.

Table 2.4 uses a GOTO in line 80 in a similar way. After printing an error message (if a name containing more than four characters has been entered), the program returns to the input line (line 30):

```
60 PRINT "NAME TOO LONG (ENTER"
70 PRINT "4 CHARACTERS ONLY)"
80 GOTO 30
```

IF . . . THEN

The IF . . . THEN statement has the form:

IF relational expression THEN line number (or statement). The relational expression compares two values and branches to the line number or executes the statement after THEN if the comparison is *true* (i.e. the relational expression is true). If it is not true, then the next statement after the IF . . . THEN statement is executed. For example, Table 2.1 contains:

```
40 IF C$ = "M" THEN 70
50 R=X+Y+Z
```

If the string variable C$ contains the character "M", then line 70, which multiplies the three variables X, Y and Z, is executed, otherwise line 50 will be executed next.

Table 3.1 contains a different type of relational expression in line 50:

```
50 IF LEN (P$)<> 3 THEN 20
```

<> means 'not equal to'.

Table 4.1 shows an example of a statement after THEN in line 165:

```
165 IF A$ = "N" THEN END
```

INPUT

The INPUT statement allows the program to obtain data for variables when the program is run. When the program reaches an INPUT statement, it will display a question mark (?) on the screen and wait for data to be entered from the keyboard. The data from the keyboard should be terminated by pressing the RETURN key. The INPUT statement is followed by a variable list, and the data from the keyboard is stored in the variables in sequence, as shown in:

10 INPUT A,B,C

Line 10 will require three numeric values to be entered from the keyboard. They can be entered on separate lines by pressing the RETURN key after each value or they can be entered on one line by separating the values with commas.

The equivalent of the PRINT statement can be incorporated within quotes in an INPUT statement but must be separated from the input variable list by a semi-colon (;). This is illustrated in Table 4.9:

30 INPUT "STARTING COLOUR (W/B)";C$

INPUT#

This statement is used for obtaining data from a previously OPENed file. The general form of the statement is:

INPUT# file number, variable list

Table 8.2 uses an INPUT# statement to read in details of the MEMBERS file:

200 INPUT# 1,RN$,S$,F$,A1$,A2$,A3$,TN$,IN$

In this case, the file MEMBERS was OPENed for reading at line 70 and given a file number of 1:

70 OPEN 1,1,0,"MEMBERS"

(see also OPEN).

INT

This function returns the integer value of a number contained in a variable. For example: x = INT(12.76) sets x equal to 12.

If the INT function is to be used for rounding up or down, the form is:

x = INT(N + 0.5)

when x will equal 13 when N = 12.76
and x will equal 12 when N = 12.32.

This form of expression has been used in Table 5.1 in line 240:

240 L=INT(15*N(D)/MAX+0.5)

In this program, MAX has been set to the maximum value of N(D) so that for any particular value of N(D) the result of N(D)/MAX lies between 0 and 1. Multiplying by 15 scales the result up to lie between 0 and 15. As L needs to be set to the integer value nearest the result, 0.5 is added to the result prior to taking the integer value.

The INT function can be used to calcuate the decimal part of a variable. For example:

x = Y − INT(Y)

would set x to 0.76 if Y were 12.76.

The conversion of a time duration (D) expressed in 1/60th of a second into minutes (M) and seconds (S) is carried out in Table 4.9 by using the INT function:

80 M=INT(D/3600)
90 S=INT(D/60)−60*M

The number of minutes is calculated in line 80 by dividing D by 3600 (i.e. 60 × 60) and dropping the decimal part of the result. In line 90, INT(D/60) is the total number of seconds represented by D. The total number of seconds contained in the minutes (M) is 60*M. Therefore, after calculating the minutes (M), the number of seconds remaining is INT(D/60)−60*M.

LEFT$

LEFT$(X$,N) returns a string containing the N leftmost characters of the string X$. For example:

10 A$="COMPUTER"
20 B$=LEFT$(A$,3)

will set B$ to "COM".

LEFT$ has been used in Table 7.1 to cause the program to respond to the first letter of any keyboard entry:

```
40 INPUT R$
50 IF LEFT$(R$,1)="C" THEN S=+K
60 IF LEFT$(R$,1)="D"THEN S=−K
65 IF LEFT$(R$,1)< CHR$(67) THEN 30
66 IF LEFT$(R$,1)> CHR$(68) THEN 30
```

If the first character of R$ is "C" then line 50 sets s to +K; if the first character is "D" then line 60 sets s to −K. If the first character is outside the ASCII code number range 67 or 68 (i.e. C or D), lines 65 or 66 send the program back to line 30.

LEN

LEN (A$) returns the number of characters (or 'length') contained in the string A$, as in:

```
10 A$="COMPUTER"
20 L=LEN(A$)
```

This will result in L being set to 8.

Table 2.4 uses the LEN function to check that the name of a fizzy drink (N$) is not more than four characters in length:

```
50 IF LEN (N$(K) )<=4 THEN 90
```

MID$

MID$(A$,S,N) returns a string containing N number of characters starting from a character within A$ specified by s. If N is omitted, that is, if MID$(A$,S) is used, then the string returned will start at the character specified by s and finish at the end of the string A$. For example:

```
10 A$="COMPUTER"
20 B$=MID$(A$,4,3)
30 C$=MID$(A$,7)
```

will set B$ to "PUT" and C$ to "ER".

The MID$ function has been used in Table 4.7 within a loop to compare successive characters in two strings (X$ and Z$):

```
295 FOR I = 1 TO 3
300 IF MID$(X$,I,1) = MID$(Z$,I,1) THEN 335
...
...
...
340 NEXT I
```

ON . . . GOSUB

The command ON X GOSUB 200,300,400 causes the program to evaluate the variable x and if the result is 1 to execute the subroutine at the first line number (200), if 2 the subroutine at the second line number (300), etc. If the value of x is negative, zero or greater than the list of line numbers (i.e. three in the above example), the program passes to the next line. On return from a subroutine, the next line to be executed will be the one immediately after the ON . . . GOSUB.

This command has been used in Table 8.1:

```
430 PRINT "FIELD TO BE CORRECTED"
435 INPUT L
440 ON L GOSUB 500,510,520,530,540,550,560,570
450 GOTO 400
```

In this application, the different subroutines allow the appropriate data entry to be corrected.

ON . . . GOTO

The command ON . . . GOTO operates in a similar way to ON . . . GOSUB, the difference being that as the branching is *not* to a subroutine the program does not return automatically to the line after the ON . . . GOTO.

An example of the use of this command (from Table 3.1) is:

```
1010 ON C GOTO 1100,1200,1300,20
```

which will cause branching to either lines 1100, 1200, 1300 or 20 depending on whether c has the value 1, 2, 3 or 4.

OPEN

Any files to be used in a program need to be declared before use. For example, the line:

70 OPEN 1,1,1,"MEMBERS"

taken from Table 8.1, indicates that a file named "MEMBERS" will be referred to subsequently as file 1 and is located on device 1. The third 1 indicates that the file is to be written to (to read a file the third number would be 0). Line 70 in Table 8.2 declares that this same file is to be read:

70 OPEN 1,1,0,"MEMBERS"

Files should be closed after processing, so in both programs there are CLOSE statements (line 700, Table 8.1, and line 300, Table 8.2).

Writing to a file and reading a file is achieved by the use of PRINT# and INPUT# statements (see separate entries).

PEEK

PEEK examines a specified memory location and returns the character code of the contents, that is, a number from 0 to 255.

The robot program (Table 6.1) uses this function to examine the contents of the screen position (variable R) that the robot is about to move into:

```
1035 IF PEEK(R)=32 THEN 1050
1040 IF PEEK(R)=96 THEN 1050
1045 K=2:GOTO 2000
```

If the value found is 32 or 96 (lines 1035 and 1040) then the robot can move into this position as 32 and 96 are screen character codes for a space. If the values 32 or 96 are *not* found, the program continues to line 1045 where K is set to 2, which is used in a later line to activate the message YOU HAVE CRASHED.

POKE

POKE stores a number between 0 and 255 in a specified memory location. For the Commodore VIC, the screen and border colours can be changed by POKEing memory location 36879. For example, the POKE in Table 4.2, line 5, i.e. POKE 36879,216 produces a light green screen and a black border.

Characters can be POKEd to the screen by using a POKE number that represents the required screen position. The number 7680 represents the screen home (top leftmost) position; other positions are related to this number by their displacement from the home position. The colour of any character POKEd to the screen is controlled by POKEing a value, one less than the number shown on the colour keys of the VIC, to colour memory locations. The equivalent colour memory location for the home position is 38400, the displacement being the same as that for the character code. An example of the use of these POKEs (from Table 4.2) is:

1000 POKE 8039,24:POKE 38759,0

Line 1000 POKEs the character x (screen code 24) to screen position 8039 which is 359 cursor positions from the home position (i.e. 8039 − 7680). The colour of the x is black because zero is used in POKE 38759,0. Note that 38759 is also 359 cursor positions from the colour home position, 38400.

The three tone generators and noise generator are activated by POKEing to memory locations 36874, 36875, 36876, 36877. The sound level of these is set by POKEing a value between 0 and 15 to memory location 36878. Table 4.6 uses these POKEs to produce a sound effect, i.e.

4010 POKE 36877,140

. . .

4030 POKE 36878,L

Line 4010 sets the noise generator to produce a particular sound while 4030 varies its volume according to the value of L.

PRINT

The PRINT statement is used to display messages and the contents of variables on the screen. Messages to be displayed are enclosed in quotation marks:

10 PRINT "ENTER A FOR ADD"

Messages and variables can be included in the same line but must be separated by a comma or a semi-colon (known as 'delimiters'), as illustrated by Table 2.1:

90 PRINT "RESULT =";R

Using a semi-colon as a delimiter causes the following output (in this case, the value of R) to be displayed from the next screen position along the line. For the Commodore VIC-20, if a comma is used, the output following is displayed from the middle of the screen onwards, or at the start of the next line if the cursor is already past the middle of the screen.

The cursor can also be positioned within a PRINT statement by the use of the TAB command (see TAB).

A semi-colon at the end of a PRINT statement causes the *next* PRINT statement executed to produce output as a *continuation* of that produced by the previous PRINT statement. For example, the following lines taken from the patterns program (Table 5.4) output a row of sixteen coloured rectangles using space characters in reverse video:

220 FOR P=1 TO 16
230 PRINT O$(P,L)" ▚ ";
240 NEXT P

PRINT#

The PRINT# statement is used to write to a cassette file using the form, PRINT# file number. The file should be already OPENed. Table 8.1 illustrates the use of the PRINT# statement:

80 PRINT # 1,DS$

This line writes the contents of DS$ (the date as a string) to the MEMBERS file (OPENed in line 70).

When several variables are written to a file with a single PRINT# line, the variables must be separated on the file by commas, so that any subsequent INPUT# can read them back individually. This is done by writing commas as strings between each variable, as in:

```
600 PRINT# 1,RN$;",";S$;",";F$;",";A1$;",";A2$;
610 PRINT# 1,",";A3$;",";TN$;",";IN$
```

READ

The READ statement causes the computer to store the *next* value in a series of DATA lines in the variable specified. For example, the program lines:

```
10 READ A,B
20 READ C
30 DATA 10,27,1.5
```

would cause A to be set to 10, B to 27 and C to 1.5.

String variables can be read in a similar manner. Lines 15 to 27 in Table 4.1 illustrate the reading of twenty-six string values (the letters A to Z) and storing them in the array X$ by means of a FOR . . . NEXT loop:

```
15 FOR I=1 TO 26
20 READ X$(I):NEXT I
25 DATA A,B,C,D,E,F,G,H,I,J,K,L,M
27 DATA N,O,P,Q,R,S,T,U,V,W,X,Y,Z
```

REM

The REM statement allows the programmer to include lines containing remarks. The computer does not execute anything that follows REM on a line. Using REM lines helps to make the program understandable to the reader. Table 3.1 contains several REM lines to distinguish parts of the program where otherwise the coding is similar:

```
1100 REM BIRTHDAYS
1200 REM ARRANGEMENTS
1300 REM TERM DATES
```

RETURN

A RETURN statement is required for each subroutine. A GOSUB causes the program to branch to the specified line number and continue executing from that line until a RETURN is encountered (see GOSUB).

RND

RND is a function that returns a randomly generated number lying between 0 and 1. For example, the following line simulates the throw of a dice:

```
10 D=INT(RND(3)*6)+1
```

The RND(3) in the line generates a random number between 0 and 1. The value 3 produces a particular sequence of pseudo-random numbers; a different value, for example 1, would produce a different sequence. The number is scaled up by multiplying by 6 so that the result so far could be a number from 0 up to, but not including 6, that is, 5.99999. The integer of this result is therefore a whole number between 0 and 5. By adding 1 the result will be a whole number from 1 to 6, representing a throw of a dice.

Table 4.1 uses the RND function to choose one letter of the alphabet at random from a list of the twenty-six letters stored in X$:

```
95 X=INT(RND(1)*26)+1
. . .
105 PRINT"PRESS KEY";"    ''';X$(X);"''''
```

STEP

STEP can be used as part of a FOR . . . NEXT statement (see FOR . . . NEXT).

STR$

This function converts a numeric value stored in a variable to a string that is the equivalent of its PRINTed form, e.g.

```
10 D=24
20 E$="TH."
30 D$=STR$(D)
40 PRINT D$;E$
```

Line 40 will result in 24TH. being displayed on the screen. The STR$ function is used in Table 4.7 to convert a number so that it can be processed as a string:

```
120 Z$=MID$(STR$(INT(RND(1)*889)+111),2)
```

TAB

TAB(X) is used in a PRINT statement to space to column number X, that is, it causes the cursor to move to this column, where the first column in a line is column zero. The TAB function is separated in a PRINT list by the semi-colon delimiter, as in:

```
10 PRINT "NAME";TAB(15);"TEAM"
```

Line 10 produces headings with NAME displayed at column 0 (the first column) onwards and TEAM at column 15 (i.e. the 16th column) onwards.

Table 2.4 uses the TAB function to PRINT lines of output displayed neatly in four columns:

```
220 PRINT N$(L);TAB(4);S(L);
225 PRINT TAB(11);P(L);TAB(16);C
```

TI

TI is the name of a variable that is automatically increased by one every 1/60th of a second. It starts at zero when the VIC is switched on. Differences in the value stored in TI at various stages of a program can be used to measure time intervals. For example, in

```
10 N=TI
...
...
...
90 T=TI
100 S=(T−N)/60
```

line 100 calculates the difference between values stored in TI at two stages in a program run (these are stored in N and T at lines 10 and 90) and divides this by 60 to obtain the result in seconds.

Table 4.1 uses TI to calculate the time taken between two parts of the program separated only by a GET statement. This time difference represents the time (T) taken to respond correctly to the GET statement:

```
110 A=TI
115 GET A$:IF A$<>X$(X) THEN 115
120 B=TI
125 T=INT((B−A)/60*10)/10
```

Line 125 truncates the time interval (that is, drops unnecessary decimal places), so that the result is in seconds with one decimal place.

VAL

This function converts a string into a number, as in:

```
10 X=VAL("123")
```

Line 10 causes the value 123 to be stored in X. Note that the VAL function converts a string from left to right. The conversion is terminated when a non-numeric character is found:

```
20 X=VAL("123AB4")
```

In line 20, X will contain 123; the 4 is not reached as the conversion is terminated at A, and characters AB4 are lost.

If the first character of the VAL string (A$, for example) is not +, −, $ or a digit, then VAL(A$) = 0. This was used in the noughts and crosses program (Table 4.2) to test for a valid move:

```
5010 GET A$:IF A$="" THEN 5010
5020 IF VAL(A$)=0 THEN 5010
5030 N=VAL(A$)
5040 IF B(N)<>0 THEN 5010
```

After a character has been entered from the keyboard (line 5010), it is tested in line 5020 for zero. Strictly speaking, we should also test for $+$, $-$ and $, in case one of these keys has been pressed by mistake, as the test allows only for the other non-numeric characters and zero (we have assumed that it is more likely that these characters could be pressed by mistake). Assuming one of the digits 1 to 9 has been pressed at line 5010, then this value is stored in N at line 5030. Line 5040 tests to make sure that the selected grid square is empty, that is, B(N) is equal to 0, otherwise the move is not accepted and the program returns to line 5010 to wait for another move.

Table 3.1 uses the VAL function to store two digits of a number that has been entered as a string of three characters (P$):

```
60 V=VAL(MID$(P$,1,1))
70 C=VAL(MID$(P$,2,1))
```

Special Features

Clear screen

The screen can be cleared and the cursor moved to the home position by use of the CLR key. This key can be used within quotes in a string in a program. When listed, the use of this key is indicated by a heart character in reverse video.

An example of the clear screen character can be found in line 110, Table 3.1.

Colon (:)

The colon (:) is used to separate statements when they are written on one line, as in:

10 FOR I = I TO 10:READ X(I):NEXT I

Line 10 consists of three statements forming a FOR . . . NEXT loop.

Table 4.1 uses a colon to allow a GET delay loop to be written on one line:

115 GET A$:IF A$<>X$(X) THEN 115

Colour control

The colour of the border, screen and characters for the Commodore VIC can be controlled by the use of the POKE command (see POKE).

The colour of characters can also be controlled by keying the colour control keys within quotes in statements wherever a string would be acceptable. Within a program, listing the use of the colour control keys is shown by special character symbols.

Table 5.4 uses a string (A$) that consists of all eight colour characters:

30 A$="■◆◥▲▓▒▀"

Cursor control

The cursor can be moved in a program by placing cursor control movements within strings as part of a statement. The five cursor movements (*up, down, left, right*) and *home* are represented by special characters. For example, in Table 5.4:

40 PRINT"▓◫◫◫"

causes the cursor to move to the *home* position and then *down* three lines prior to displaying the question mark (?) associated with the INPUT statement.

Table 8.1 uses cursor control within strings for its INPUT subroutines at lines 510 to 570.

Graphics characters

Any of the graphics symbols on the keyboard can be included within strings and used within PRINT statements to form charts, diagrams and pictures on the screen.

Table 4.2 uses graphics characters to produce a noughts and crosses board on the screen by a series of PRINT statements (lines 30 to 70).

Reverse video

Any screen characters can be displayed in reverse video, that is, background and foreground colours reversed by the use of the RVS ON key. This mode is turned off by the use of the RVS OFF key. The key can be used within quotes in a string. When listed, the use of the keys is indicated in the program by special characters.

Line 20 of Table 5.1 stores a reverse bar of spaces in the variable B$.

Sound

The tone and noise generators are turned on and off and their volume controlled by the use of POKE statements (see POKE).

Appendix B

Hints on converting programs to run on different micro-computers

Introduction

The programs given in this book all run on the Commodore VIC microcomputer. If you are using a different micro-computer, you will need to find out which BASIC statements are available on your machine. You can do this by referring to the user manual which is supplied with the microcomputer.

There are particular things you should look for, depending on the microcomputer you are using. In the space allowed, we can point out only a few important differences between the BASIC used for the VIC programs described in this book and the BASIC available on some of the other popular micro-computers. We have included one converted program or the necessary changes to a program in this book for each machine mentioned. This will give you a start, and it shouldn't be long before you have mastered your machine and found out its facilities.

Apple microcomputer using Applesoft BASIC

The main differences are in the use of cursor controls in program statements and graphics (there are no graphics keys). There are special BASIC commands for drawing points and lines, but you cannot PEEK or POKE characters to the screen. Applesoft BASIC has built-in high-resolution graphics functions. Colour commands may be used with a colour television monitor.

Table B.1   Caterpillar program for the Apple microcomputer

```
10 L$(1)="<***O"
20 L$(2)="<**O"
30 S$="                              "
40 K=2:X=-1:Z=1
110 FOR I=1 TO 34
112 FOR L=1 TO 2
115 HOME
118 VTAB 5
120 PRINT LEFT$(S$,I);L$(K)
125 FOR D=1 TO 400:NEXT D
130 Z=Z*X
140 K=K+Z
145 NEXT L
150 NEXT I
```

The Caterpillar program given in Table B.1 illustrates how you can clear the screen and move the cursor within a program. The graphics symbol previously used in lines 10 and 20 of the original program (Table 5.3) has been replaced by an asterisk. The wider width of screen has been taken into account in lines 30 and 110. Line 115 clears the screen and line 118 tabs the cursor vertically down five lines. The delay loop in line 125 has been changed to match the speed of execution of the Apple.

BBC microcomputer (Model A)

The Patterns program (Table 5.4) has been converted to run on a BBC model A microcomputer using mode 5, which gives a four-colour display. Additional display modes are available on the model B version.

As *different* colours cannot be held directly in strings, the revised program adopts a slightly different approach to producing a pattern. Instead of a 16 × 16 array of *colours* being built up by the program, a 16 × 16 array of *numbers* is built up, using the same logic. The colour is introduced at the printing stage when the number in the array is interpreted as a colour. Thus, the program follows very similar logic but no string variables are used.

Revised program

Table B.2 Patterns program for the BBC microcomputer (Model A)

```
10 DIM C(8),D(8),O(16,16)
15 MODE 5
20 CLS
40 PRINT TAB(5,8)
50 FOR I=1 TO 8
60 N=INT(RND(1)*4)+128
70 C(I)=N
80 D(I)=N
90 NEXT I
100 FOR L=1 TO 8
110 D(1)=C(L)
120 FOR P=8 TO 1 STEP -1
130 O(P,L)=D(P)
140 O(17-P,L)=D(P)
150 O(P,17-L)=D(P)
160 O(17-P,17-L)=D(P)
170 D(P)=D(P-1)
180 NEXT P
190 NEXT L
200 FOR L=1 TO 16
210 PRINT " ";
220 FOR P=1 TO 16
225 COLOUR O(P,L)
230 PRINT " ";
240 NEXT P
245 COLOUR 128
250 PRINT
260 NEXT L
270 GOTO 40
```

The revised Patterns program is shown in Table B.2. Line 10 specifies an o numeric array in place of o$. In addition, the arrays c$ (now c) and D$ (now D) need to be dimensioned, even though they are less than 10.

The additional line 15 puts the microcomputer into mode

5. Line 20 clears the screen. The cursor is positioned in line 40 by using a two-dimensional TAB statement. This positions the cursor at column 5, line 8.

Random numbers to represent colours are generated in line 60. The random number function is multiplied by 4 instead of 8 because there are only four colours in mode 5. The resulting number (between 0 and 3) would represent a *foreground colour*. To print a space as a coloured block, the *background colour* (to the text) is used. The background colours are specified by adding 128 to their equivalent foreground colour codes. Hence, N becomes a randomly generated background colour value (between 128 and 131). The colours are:

128　black
129　red
130　yellow
131　white

These numbers are assigned in the loop to C(I) and D(I) at lines 70 and 80 respectively.

Lines 100 to 190 form a loop that sets up the pattern in array O. In this case, the array contains a numeric pattern.

The pattern is printed out within the loop from line 200 to line 260. The original print statement at line 230 is replaced by two lines. Line 225 specifies the background colour by using the current value of array O. Line 230 prints a space using this background colour. At the end of each line of the pattern (that is, on leaving the FOR P . . . NEXT P loop), the background colour is reset to black (line 245) to preserve the border around the pattern.

Commodore PET microcomputer

You will find that the VIC programs are compatible with PET BASIC apart from the colour and sound facilities, which are not available on the PET, and the memory locations used in POKE (or PEEK) statements.

For example, the Noughts and Crosses program, given in

Table 4.2, can easily be converted for running on the PET by making the following changes:

1 Remove line 5, which changes the screen and border colour combination and the colour of the displayed characters on the VIC.

2 Change lines 80 and 85 to specify the PET screen home memory location as 32768 with displacements (D) allowing for a 40-column PET screen:

80 READ D:P(I)=32768+D
85 DATA 161,164,167,281,284,287,401,404,407

3 Change lines 1000 and 2000 to give the appropriate PET screen memory locations:

1000 POKE 33417,24
2000 POKE 33417,15

You need to make similar changes to the Find the Treasure program shown in Table 4.4, Chapter 4. For this program you must leave out the explosion subroutine, given in Table 4.6, and line 317, which branches to this subroutine.

Sharp microcomputer

Sharp BASIC is very similar to the BASIC used in this book. To modify the Caterpillar program (Table 5.3) only one additional line is necessary. This is to dimension the string L$, that is:

5 DIM L$(2)

As the screen is 40 characters wide, line 100 can be changed to FOR I=1 TO 34, in which case the string of spaces set up in line 30 needs to be increased to 34 spaces.

Sharp PEEKs *and* POKEs

The principles of PEEKing and POKEing on the Sharp are similar to those described in this book, but the character code numbers will be different. A detailed list of the display and special character codes is given in the Sharp manual.

The top left-hand position of the screen is location 53248 and there are 0 to 999 possible displacements from this position (that is, 40 characters $\times$ 25 lines). A character can be POKEd to any displacement by:

POKE 53248+x,y

where x is the required displacement and y is the screen character code.

Character codes for the special cursor control key are:

cursor down CHR$(193)
cursor up CHR$(194)
cursor right CHR$(195)
cursor left CHR$(196)
cursor home CHR$(197)
clear screen CHR$(198)

Sinclair zx81 microcomputer

The main things to watch are the use of character strings and functions, graphics and avoiding the use of some BASIC commands and facilities which are not available on the zx81.

Character strings and functions

Character strings need to be stored in arrays and therefore require a DIM statement.

Only LEN, VAL and STR$ are available as string functions. However, you can 'slice' strings by specifying:

string expression (start TO finish)
e.g. "TEACHER"(2 TO 5)="EACH"

Graphics

There are 22 graphics symbols (including space) that can be entered via the keyboard or used via the CHR$ function. You cannot PEEK or POKE to the screen.

Pictures can be produced on the screen by using the PLOT and UNPLOT statements by referring to the horizontal and vertical distances from the bottom left-hand corner of the screen measured in pixels. The screen consists of 64 pixels horizontally (0 to 63) and 44 pixels vertically (0 to 43). A character is normally made up of 2×2 pixels.

For example, PLOT 10,20 displays a black pixel, 10 pixels up and 20 pixels along. The UNPLOT statement blanks out a black pixel at the specified co-ordinate.

READ, DATA

These cannot be used. Use LET statements to assign values to variables where appropriate.

Example program

Table B.3   Caterpillar program for the Sinclair zx81 micro-computer

```
 5 DIM L$(2,6)
10 LET L$(1)=" <***Q"
20 LET L$(2)=" <**Q"
40 LET K=2
50 LET X=-1
60 LET Z=1
110 FOR I=1 TO 24
112 FOR L=1 TO 2
120 PRINT AT 5,I;L$(K)
125 FOR D=1 TO 5
128 NEXT D
130 LET Z=Z*X
140 LET K=K+Z
145 NEXT L
150 NEXT I
```

A version of the Caterpillar program, given in Table 5.3, is shown in Table B.3. Note that the DIM statement in line 5 is used to allocate storage for two strings, each of six characters. Line 40 in the VIC program has been rewritten over lines 40, 50 and 60, since several statements cannot be separated by colons on one line. Lines 30 and 115 of the VIC program are not required, since a PRINT AT statement has been used in line 120 to cause the caterpillar to move along row 5 as the variable I is increased by the FOR . . . NEXT loop. I now goes from 1 to 24 to take into account the larger screen size on the zx81. Execution is relatively slow, so the delay loop (lines 125 and 128) has been reduced from 500 to 5.

Appendix C

Glossary of computer terms

Accumulator: a storage location in which arithmetic results are accumulated

Acoustic coupler: a device attached to a portable terminal or computer into which a telephone handset is inserted to allow information to be passed acoustically over the telephone line to a remote computer system

A/D converter: analog/digital converter; converts analog (continuous) signals, usually from sensors measuring temperature, voltage, etc., to digital (binary) signals for processing by a computer

Address: the unique identification of a specific storage location in the computer's memory

ALU: the arithmetic and logic unit of the central processor which performs calculations and compares values during the processing of data

ASCII: American Standard Code for Information Interchange by which characters (for example, letters, punctuation and numerals) are coded into binary

Assembler: a program that converts a low-level language program into machine code

Backing storage: all forms of storage that are external to the main store

Back-up copy: the copy of a program or data which is made on disk or tape in case the original becomes damaged or altered accidentally

Bar code: a code represented by a succession of printed bars found particularly on supermarket items; the code is 'read' optically by passing a sensing pen connected to a computer over the lines

BASIC: Beginners All-purpose Symbolic Instruction Code, a high-level programming language

Binary notation: the representation of decimal numbers using only the 0s and 1s of the mathematical system known as the binary code

Bit: a *bi*nary digi*t*

Byte: a group of binary digits, usually eight bits

CAD: computer-aided design

Ceefax: a videotex system broadcast by the BBC

Central processing unit: the unit comprised of the ALU, control unit and memory

Character: a particular alphanumeric symbol such as a letter of the alphabet, punctuation mark or numeral

Chip: an electronic circuit produced on a single piece of semi-conductor based material, for example, silicon; also called a micro-chip, silicon chip, integrated circuit

Clock: the circuit that produces regular electronic pulses that enable the operation of all units of a computer to be synchronized

Compiler: a program that is loaded into main memory to convert a program written in a high-level language to machine code

Control unit: that part of the central processing unit which accesses program instructions, interprets them, and controls their execution

cpu: see central processing unit

Cursor: a marker on the vdu screen which indicates where the next character will be displayed

d/a converter: converts digital to analog signals (see also a/d converter)

Daisywheel printer: a printer that has the character set on the circumference of a spinning wheel which moves across the paper

Data base: a systematic, interrelated set of data files that allows combinations of the data to be selected as requested by different users

Delimiter: the character used to separate items of data when input or stored in files; a comma is often used

Disk: a backing storage device that has information stored magnetically on concentric tracks over the surfaces of the disk

Dumping: the copying of information from the computer to backing store as a security measure

EPROM: Erasable Programmable Read Only Memory; an erasable form of PROM

Execution: the processing by the computer of programmed instructions

Expression: the name given to an algebraic or logical relationship

Field: a sub-division of a record

File: an organized set of records

Floppy disk: a single pliable disk, usually contained in a protective sleeve, used for storing programs and data

Flowchart: a chart showing the sequence of logic of a computer program

Hardware: the physical devices making up a computer system, as opposed to the software

High-level language: a term applied to a programming language in which each instruction corresponds to several machine code instructions; such a language often consists of English words and mathematical symbols

Integrated circuit (IC): see chip

Interpreter: a program that is loaded into main memory, or available in ROM, to convert instructions written in a high-level programming language to machine code; an interpreter is different from a compiler since each instruction is executed immediately after it has been translated into machine code

IPS: Information Providers – the providers of information in a videotex system

Joystick: a hand-held stick that pivots at its base; the movement of the stick causes a corresponding movement in the same direction of a character on the VDU screen

Line printer: a printer on a computer system that prints a line at a time

Local area network (LAN): the interconnection of several computers and associated devices within local distances, which can communicate with each other

Low-level language: a programming language that is closer to machine code than a high-level language is; programs generally are more difficult to write in a low-level language than they are in a high-level language, but usually run faster

Machine code: the binary instruction code used by the central processor in a particular machine

Magnetic stripe: a stripe of magnetic material, sometimes added to the price label of items, encoded and scanned by a hand-held pen (also known as a wand)

Magnetic tape: a type of backing storage on which information is stored magnetically; the tape may be in cassette form or spooled for reel-to-reel use

Main store: the central storage area coupled directly to the CPU which is used for holding the operating system and the program instructions to be executed as well as the data currently being processed

MICR: Magnetic Ink Character Recognition code, for example, printed along the bottom of cheques using ink that can be magnetized so that coding can be read directly into a computer system

Microprocessor: a central processing unit designed as a single chip used in microcomputers and in the control system of some industrial and domestic equipment

Modem: a modulator-demodulator; a device used to convert digital signals into audio signals (modulate) before transmission over, for example, a telephone line, and to convert received audio signals into digital form (demodulate) for use by a computer system

OCR: Optical Character Recognition; a method used to input printed characters into a computer system by scanning them with light-sensitive heads that 'read' each character

Operating system: a program used to control the functioning of a computer system

Oracle: a videotex system broadcast by commercial television

Package: a program and associated documentation developed for an application

Password: a unique sequence of characters that needs to be entered at a terminal before a user can gain access to a computer

Peripheral: the name given to any input or output device that can be connected to the main memory and CPU of any computer system

POS: Point Of Sale terminal; a terminal which looks like a cash register and is used to record sales information for transmission to a computer

Prestel: a videotex system transmitted over the public telephone system and displayed on the screen of an adapted television set by means of a direct link between the telephone and the television

Program: a sequence of instructions that cause the computer to perform the necessary processing for a given application

PROM: Programmable Read Only Memory; a programmable form of ROM

RAM: Random Access Memory (read-addressable memory); a chip that forms part of the main memory of a computer and that is used for holding programs and data read in from peripheral devices; the contents of RAM are lost when the power to the computer is switched off

Record: a related set of data; the items of data are known as fields and a collection of records is referred to as a file

Registers: specific storage areas in the CPU and main memory used to control the functioning of the computer and to provide information on the present state of the processing during a computer run

ROM: Read Only Memory; a chip used for storing programs or data that need to be permanently incorporated into a computer; ROM retains its contents when the power to the computer is switched off

Secondary storage: see backing storage

Software: a term applied to programs used by computer hardware

Source program: a program as originally written in a high- or low-level language before the computer translates it into machine code

String: a sequence of characters, for example, letters, punctuation and numerals

Subroutine: a group of program instructions which can be entered from several points of the program; after execution of these instructions, control returns to the program instruction following the instruction which called the subroutine

Systems analysis: the analysis of a proposed computer application that leads to the design of suitable software to be used with associated hardware

Telesoftware: the provision of software by means of teletex or viewdata

Teletext: the transmission of text and diagrammatic information, broadcast by television channels, that can be received by modified television sets

Terminal: an input-output device linked to a computer that is used for entry and processing of programs and data; some terminals may be input only or output only devices

Time-sharing: the use of a computer system by several users, apparently simultaneously and independently

vdu: Visual Display Unit; a device like a television screen that displays output from a computer and input if an input device, such as a keyboard, is connected

Verify: the term applied to the checking of data in a computer system

Videotex: the transmission of computer-based text and diagrammatic information that can be displayed on modified television sets; the transmission may be via telephone lines

Viewdata: an alternative term for videotex

Wand: the name given to a hand-held 'pen' that is passed over bar-coded or magnetic-stripe labels; the pen 'reads' the labels and passes the information to the computer

Winchester disk: a hard-disk unit, sealed into a case, used as an alternative to floppy disks

Word: the number of bits that can be handled by a computer in a single step; the size of the word depends on the computer being used

Index